Par and Yardage

Hole	Par	Yardage	Hole	Par	Yardage
1	4	433	10	4	450
2	5	523	11	4	398
3	3	194	12	5	560
4	4	430	13	3	170
5	4	455	14	4	471
6	4	356	15	4	400
7	4	405	16	4	403
8	4	440	17	3	200
9	3	220	18	4	465
	35	3,456		35	3,518
				70	6,974

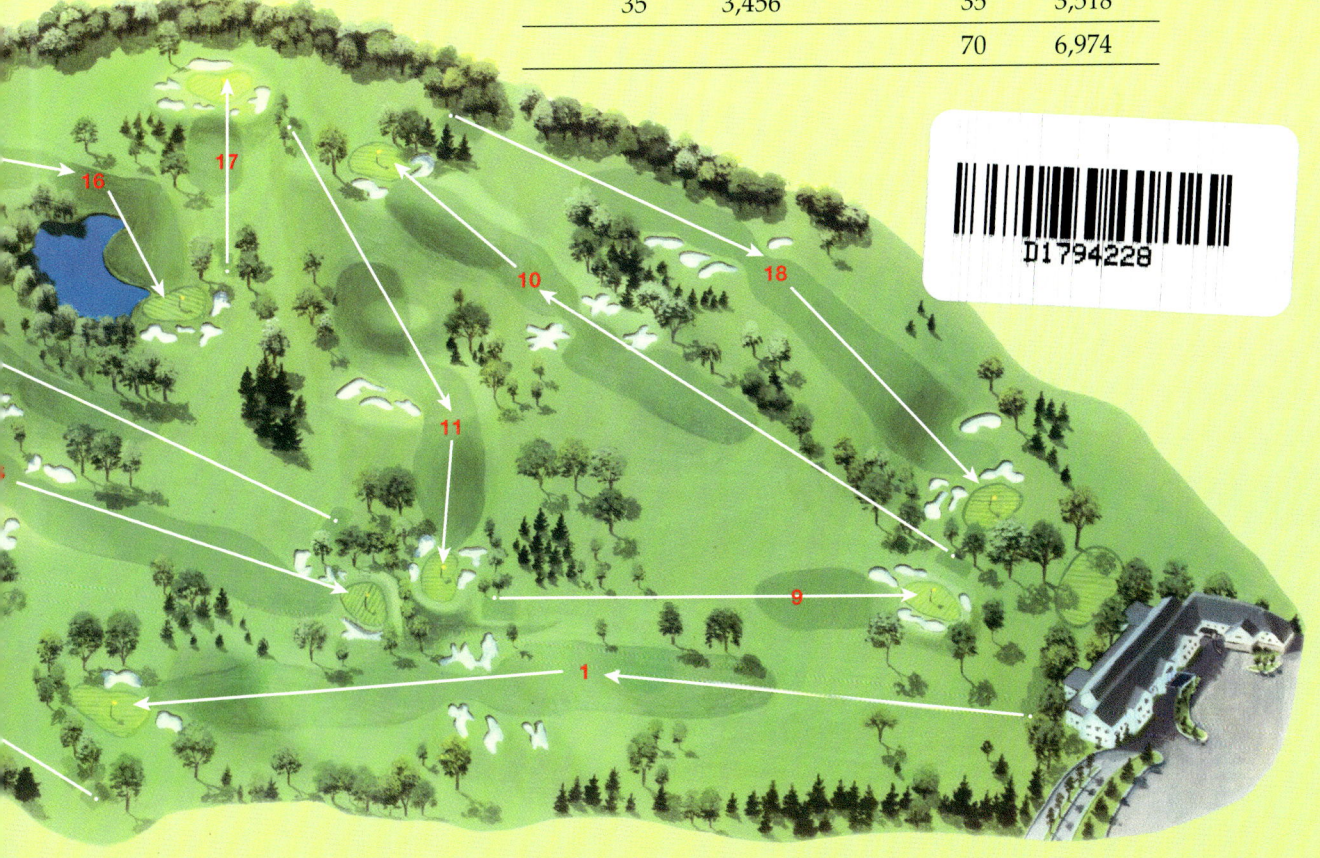

ISBN 1-878843-16-8

©1996 United States Golf Association®
Golf House, Far Hills, New Jersey 07931

Statistics produced by Unisys Corporation

Published by International Merchandising Corporation,
One Erieview Plaza, Cleveland, Ohio 44114

Designed and produced by Davis Design

Printed in the United States of America

Whenever the United States Golf Association brings one of its championships to the Detroit area, I have fond memories because it was there I won the 1954 Amateur at the Country Club of Detroit, my first, and the 1981 Senior Open at Oakland Hills, my most recent USGA victory.

The host of the U.S. Open for a sixth time, Oakland Hills provides with its South Course what is regarded as one of the most gruelling tests that golfers could find anywhere. Below-par scores on the South Course are few and far between.

Steve Jones was certainly deserving of his title this year, playing three fantastic rounds after starting with 74. His 204 total for the last 54 holes was just one stroke off the U.S. Open record. Others to be congratulated included runners-up Tom Lehman and Davis Love III.

This is the 12th annual commemorative book on the U.S. Open produced by our friends at Rolex Watch USA. The purpose of this book is to document the 1996 Championship in words and color photographs. I am especially pleased that all proceeds are to be directed to the USGA Members Program for activities to benefit junior golf.

Arnold Palmer

96th U.S. Open
Oakland Hills Country Club

For a sixth time, the United States Open comes to Oakland Hills. Back to the feared South Course, an icon among global golf courses. "The Monster," as characterized at the 1951 Open's trophy presentation by Ben Hogan, a steely Texan who felt more like a survivor than a conqueror despite ruling at Oakland Hills with a seven-over-par 287 score.

This was a mighty Hogan, at the apex of his post-World War II dominance. Almost any course seemed Ben's prey. Byron Nelson was a 1940s wonder, Sam Snead was a marvelous talent, but Hogan reigned as golf's king, especially in U.S. Opens.

After winning golf's toughest championship in 1948 at Riviera (Los Angeles), Ben would miss the 1949 U.S. Open due to a life-threatening car crash, head-on with a bus on a west Texas highway. But after a stunning recovery, Hogan won again in the 1950 Open at Merion (Philadelphia) and a year later achieved a personal third straight U.S. Open in 1951 at Oakland Hills.

Monster or no monster.

Hogan's victorious war with the South Course more than impressed the small, wiry sensation in the little white hat. After accepting the trophy, Ben went to the players' locker room and talked among only a few. Dan Jenkins, an extraordinary golf-writing Texan, vividly recalls Hogan terming the course as "a place so damn hard that it might drive me out of the game if I had to regularly play it for a living."

At the 1996 Open, shirts and caps and other golfing goods were sold bearing "The Monster" nickname. Hogan is widely credited with the Oakland Hills label. That's not entirely accurate. Willard Mullin, a Pulitzer Prize-winning cartoonist, had put "The Monster" tag on the South Course in newspaper artwork prior to the 1951 Open. Then, standing as Sunday's champion, Hogan said he had somehow tamed "a monster."

So many among golf's finest, from the Bobby Jones 1920s through the Jack Nicklaus wonderworks later in the century, would marvel at Oakland Hills challenges that can be frighteningly multi-dimensional.

It's a matter of length on the South Course, a par-70 venue that grinds and slithers for 6,974 yards. There is deep rough that grows above golfers' ankles in summer when the U.S. Open visits.

But, above all other well-documented examinations provided by The Monster, there are 18 undulating, undoing, near-unreadable greens that for four generations had been bringing some of golf's most celebrated practitioners to their grass-stained knees.

Nobody knew South Course greens better than Al Watrous. Runner-up to Bobby Jones in the 1926 British Open and Oakland Hills Country Club head golf professional for 37 years, Watrous once said of his favorite lawns, "They are a very old design and when we get them to the speed demanded by modern major championships, they're almost unputtable."

Oakland Hills was originally crank-started by Norval Hawkins, sales boss for Henry Ford's monumental Model-T. It happened in 1916, as World War I continued to blaze. Detroit was yet to know its football Lions, basketball Pistons or hockey Red Wings, but Motown in 1916 did have the baseball Tigers, for whom Ty Cobb was

Dawn at Oakland Hills found Ken Green first off the tee in the 96th U.S. Open Championship.

swinging both a devastating bat and demonic spikes.

Hawkins and a wealthy chum, Joseph Mack, owner of a local print shop, gathered 46 brothers from the Detroit Athletic Club to brainstorm in quest of building a golfing temple that could rank with St. Andrews and other courses with perpetual status among the world's most respected.

Donald Ross, a Scottish wizard of golf architecture, was the sculptor of choice for a 36-hole masterpiece. Walter Hagen, a flamboyant personality with major-championship golfing skills and a Beau Brummel flair for fancy dress, would become a par-pulverizing P.T. Barnum as Oakland Hills Country Club's inaugural pro.

With such wondrous foundation, the Oakland Hills portfolio would perpetually inflate through the 20th-century generations, as a more-recognizable South Course memorably served as arena for two PGA Championships, two U.S. Senior Opens, a U.S. Women's Amateur and now a sixth U.S. Open.

When the great creator, Ross, first surveyed the 250 rolling, tree-rich Michigan farm acres in 1916, his imagination already at work on Oakland Hills, the old artist from Royal Dornoch paused to proclaim, "The Lord intended this for a golf links."

Thirty-five years later, Oakland Hills had matured to full and renowned adulthood. In preparation for that 1951 U.S. Open, the original works of Ross had undergone expansion and remolding by one of the most noted of American golf architects, Robert Trent Jones. A sharpening of The Monster's teeth. Since then, the South Course has been further refined by Arthur Hills.

Shortly after Ross finished both the South and North courses, Hagen quit as the club's first resident pro. He left to become one of the world's elite players. In 1924, The Haig would return to play the first U.S. Open awarded to Oakland Hills.

Hagen was a contender, finishing fourth. But while most eyes were on Walter as well as Jones and Gene Sarazen, a little-known Englishman, Cyril Walker, shot a nine-over-par 297 total to win by three strokes over

Past champions at Oakland Hills are recognized with commemorative plaques.

Oakland Hills was hosting its sixth U.S. Open Championship.

the great Bobby. It was six years before Jones would sweep his Grand Slam in 1930, taking both the Open and Amateur championships of the United States and Britain.

In 1937, the U.S. Open came to Oakland Hills a second time. Snead, who despite lofty lifetime golfing stature would never win the championship of his country, came agonizingly close as a 25-year-old neophyte from West Virginia.

Snead's opening-round 69 tied him atop Oakland Hills leaderboards with Denny Shute. The Slammer then shot 73 and 70, leaving him one shot behind Ed Dudley after 54 holes. Snead was in a second-place tie with Ralph Guldahl.

On the final day, Snead had an eagle three at the 537-yard 18th hole. He shot 71 for a 283 total. Guldahl was still on the course, but Sam was being backslapped by fans as the likely champion. "Sporting goods people and advertising tycoons were latching on," Snead would say years later. "Radio boys pushed microphones in my face. I was being asked to collect money for endorsing everything from corn plasters to flea powder." Fate wouldn't allow it.

Guldahl rallied. He made back-to-back birdies at the 12th and 13th holes, and finished at 281. Ralph had won by two strokes, good for a first-place paycheck of $1,000. Well-wishers, interviewers and contract bearers deserted Snead. "All at once," Sam said, "it got real lonesome. As runner-up, I had nothing." It was a feeling he would know in four U.S. Opens.

The next time the Open came to the South Course was 1951, the Hogan year. Trent Jones' renovations were hotly debated through most of the tournament. He had removed 80 of the Ross bunkers, replacing them with 60 of his own design. Fairway landing areas were pinched. The result was only two sub-par rounds were shot during four punishing days, with Hogan becoming both a championship survivor as well as a locker-room critic of The Monster.

Bobby Locke, a South African putting whiz, was the halftime leader in 1951 with 71-73–144; five strokes behind stood an imposing group that included Hogan, Tommy Bolt, Claude Harmon and Lloyd Mangrum.

The 16th hole, par four, 403 yards, was the mid-point of a tough five-hole finish.

In those days, U.S. Opens were settled by a gruelling 36-hole Sunday finish. Locke was anything but a lock. When the flatstick phenom faded, finishing third, Hogan's 287 won by two over Clayton Heafner.

Oakland Hills' next U.S. Open came in 1961. Arnold Palmer was in full bloom, winning the 1960 Open at Cherry Hills and being voted PGA Player of the Year. Jack Nicklaus was an emerging force out of Ohio State University who, at age 20, finished second to Palmer in Denver. Gary Player was another new hero as the lions came to Detroit, having won the 1961 Masters.

None of them would win.

Nicklaus, still an amateur, was an early factor with rounds of 75-69 and would wind up tied for fourth. Doug Sanders, dressing in an unsubsiding array of Kool-Aid colors, made a strong run at that 1961 Open, as did Bob Rosburg, winner of a PGA Championship who would become best known as a television golf commentator.

But when the four days of Oakland Hills golfing fire subsided in 1961, the champion was Gene Littler, a low-key, consistent Californian. They called him "The Machine" and the gentleman from San Diego shot a closing 68 to prevail on The Monster with a one-over-par 281 total. Sanders finished second, tied with Bob Goalby.

For a fifth time, the Open was contested on the Ross-Jones-Hills creation in 1985. Andy North, a 6-foot-4 fellow from Wisconsin who would win just three tournaments in his career, shot 74 on Sunday but remarkably became lord of his second U.S. Open in a seven-year span. North also won at Cherry Hills in 1978.

But the most remembered two shots (no, make that three) from the 1985 Open, one of them a huge positive and the other(s) a killer negative, were struck by Chen Tze-Chung, a longshot from Taiwan. His nickname was "T.C.," initials that would come to have a second and painful meaning for Chen.

At the outset, on his second Oakland Hills hole, the slender 26-year-old Taiwanese did something that had never happened

The 17th hole, 200 yards, provided a penultimate par-three test.

in U.S. Open history. On the 527-yard par-five, Chen muscled a three-wood second shot into the cup for a double-eagle two. Less than a dozen spectators were at greenside to witness the feat.

Chen became a huge story. His splendor was slow to evaporate. T.C., who spoke little English, had a two-stroke lead on North when the final round began. After four holes, the Chen advantage had ballooned to four. He seemed unflappable and perhaps unbeatable. Until the 457-yard fifth hole, a nasty par-four, where T.C. would splinter in infamy.

By then, his audience was massive. More than 20,000 people were watching the unexpected boy wonder from the Far East. Chen's four-iron second shot would fly well wide of the green, beneath an expansive elm tree. His third, a gambling pitch, plopped woefully short of the green, nestling into deep rough eight feet from the putting surface.

Then it happened. Chen slashed at the ball, lifting it from the grass. But then, his sand wedge would nip the flying ball a second time. A dreaded double hit. Assessed with a two-stroke penalty, his T.C. nickname would cruelly come to also mean "Two Chip." Chen wobbled to a quadruple-bogey eight.

He bogeyed the next three holes. Then, on his final U.S. Open nine, Chen would admirably rally. As if by devilish destiny, T.C. lost the tournament by a single stroke, tying with Dave Barr of Canada and Denis Watson of South Africa, one stroke behind the 279 total of North. Chen would ebb into obscurity, being recollected most of all for his U.S. Open two-hitter.

North had executed the kind of grinding, consistent, patient play it often takes to win the U.S. Open. Just like seven years before, when the former University of Florida golfer won his first Open at Cherry Hills by a single shot, making a nervy four-foot putt on the concluding green. That time he edged Dave Stockton and J.C. Snead, nephew of Sam, who won every big championship on Earth but the U.S. Open.

96th U.S. Open
Prologue

Coming to the U.S. Open, 1996 golfing success in America could be defined by three-time winner Phil Mickelson, a week of rebounding greatness for 46-year-old Tom Watson and a barrage of first-time champions on the PGA Tour.

Mickelson, noted for his short-game magic, was ablaze at year's outset, winning twice in his adopted home state of Arizona, first at Tucson and then in Phoenix. Four months later, Lefty won again in May at Dallas.

Two matters continued to haunt the gifted 25-year-old Mickelson. Despite eight PGA Tour wins, Mickelson was yet to take a major championship. A quirkier barrier involved Westerner Mickelson being yet to finish first in a professional opportunity east of the Mississippi River. To win at Oakland Hills would solve both.

Watson, after a quarter century on the Tour, was striking shots as pure as ever, but pain with his putting had prohibited the 1982 U.S. Open champion and five-time British Open winner from getting a single PGA Tour win since 1987.

He was often in contention, but Watson seemed to constantly fade due to putter failings. He missed several short putts in fin-

Phil Mickelson had three victories and led the PGA Tour money list entering the U.S. Open.

ishing second in New Orleans and was a man craving a hot streak on the greens when winding up fifth at Hilton Head.

Tom kept coming close. But he needed to win, to prove something to himself, to his rivals and to the world. Then, in May, on a mighty Ohio course built by Jack Nicklaus, the Watson dry spell would be washed away in champagne.

Tom Watson had found his putting stroke, winning the Memorial.

Kansas City's golf hero shot 14-under-par 274 to win the Memorial Tournament at Muirfield Village. His persistence, guts and tough-mindedness had paid off. Watson seemed rejuvenated in self-belief heading to the U.S. Open.

But, more than anything, the PGA Tour was producing "The New Faces of '96." A windfall for first-timers. Talent had become so deep in America that dozens of non-winners could seem about to break through.

An eruption of first-timers began at the 10th Tour stop, the Honda Classic at Coral Springs, Florida, when long-hitting Minnesotan Tim (Lumpy) Herron shot a blistering 17-under-par 271 to win.

Paul Goydos, a featured character in the best-selling John Feinstein golf book, *A Good Walk Spoiled*, lived a dream the week after Herron, winning the Bay Hill Invitational at Orlando.

Good things really can come in threes, which Scott McCarron proved in the

Prologue

Two victories made Mark O'Meara a U.S. Open favorite at Oakland Hills.

Freeport-McDermott Classic in New Orleans. For back-to-back-to-back PGA Tour weekends, first-timers had dominated.

Fred Couples broke the spell when the 1992 Masters king fended off all the Tour non-winners, putting together a whopping 18-under-par 270 to gallop away by four strokes in The Players Championship on the TPC at Sawgrass course in Ponte Vedra Beach, Florida.

But, the next week, a fourth first-time PGA Tour winner in five events would emerge with Paul Stankowski in the BellSouth Classic at Atlanta. A fifth new champion came along in early June with Steve Stricker in the Kemper Open at Potomac, Maryland.

Mark O'Meara and Mark Brooks were the two golfers other than Mickelson to be early 1996 multiple winners. O'Meara started fast, taking the year's first PGA Tour trophy in the Mercedes Championship at Carlsbad, California, and he doubled up in the Greater Greensboro Chrysler Classic in North Carolina.

Mickelson and O'Meara were in a tight one-two race for the PGA Tour money lead coming to Oakland Hills with Mickelson at $1,075,691 and O'Meara with $1,071,868. Couples was third, followed by Brooks, the winner of the Bob Hope Chrysler Classic and the Shell Houston Open. David Duval, still a non-winner on the Tour but a consistent top-10 finisher, was fifth.

Coming into the U.S. Open, while tracking week-by-week results in attempted assessment of Oakland Hills possibilities, the dominant talk continually gravitated to a Georgia tragedy rather than to any of the worldly triumphs.

Nick Faldo won his third Masters at Augusta National, but golf's global constituency was uniquely mesmerized by far more shocking news, that tournament's Sunday implosion of Greg Norman.

Admittedly ravenous for a Masters green jacket, yet to embrace any major championship on his adopted American soil, Norman tied the Masters record with 63 in Thursday's first round. He was No. 1 on the Sony Ranking and looking it.

Nick Faldo had won the 1996 Masters, and had three other top-10 finishes.

Colin Montgomerie had two top-three U.S. Open finishes and a 1996 European victory.

Greg would follow with 69-71 to lead by a strangling six strokes going into the final round. But instead of a Sunday lock, the Shark became a bedeviled, flailing, well-beaten Australian.

Norman crumbled and dunked his way to 78, limping home an astonishing five shots behind as the English precision of Faldo produced a climactic 67.

Often a tormented Grand Slam runner-up, Norman had found a new and even more excruciating way to lose. But, in the aftermath, the Shark would exude a remarkable calm, a wealth of patience and a load of style. Even in disintegrating defeat, Norman would hear near-unsubsiding public and media cheers for his post-Masters deportment.

Norman jump-started his American schedule with a Miami knockout, shooting 19-under-par 269 in the Doral-Ryder Open, winning by two over Vijay Singh and Michael Bradley.

In the hours before the Open teeoff at Oakland Hills, two of the game's more popular figures withdrew due to medical reasons. Couples was befelled by chronic back problems and two-time PGA champion Nick Price was unable to fly from his Florida home due to a sinus infection.

Price was PGA Tour Player of the Year in 1993 and 1994, winning nine tournaments, but the popular man from Zimbabwe had drawn a blank in the United States for all of 1995 and half of 1996.

Faldo, a Brit who had become an American Tour regular, backed up his Masters win with solid finishes at the Mercedes (tied for second), Buick Invitational (tied for eighth) and Honda Classic (tied for ninth). But he came to Oakland Hills knowing it would be a fight against U.S. Open history.

Only four foreign-born golfers had won America's championship since 1927. Faldo

Prologue

Ernie Els was only the fourth foreign champion since 1927 with Tommy Armour's win.

was attempting to join South Africa's Gary Player (1965), England's Tony Jacklin (1970), Australia's David Graham (1981) and South Africa's Ernie Els (1994).

Faldo had played nine U.S. Opens. Thrice he seriously contended, finishing second to Curtis Strange in a playoff at Brookline in 1988, tied for third behind Hale Irwin in 1990 at Medinah and tied for fourth in 1992 when Tom Kite won at Pebble Beach.

Norman's disaster at the Masters was in the heart of a seven-tournament run that was deeply disappointing by his standards. Prior to Augusta, Greg at Bay Hill missed his first PGA Tour cut in two years and then missed again the next week as a 36-hole casualty in The Players Championship. Following the Masters, he tied for 22nd at Hilton Head, missed the cut at the Memorial and tied for 16th at Westchester.

Along with Faldo and Australia's Norman, the most popular emerging foreign bet for Oakland Hills was Colin Montgomerie of Scotland. At 33, he had become the best player on the PGA European Tour. Monty's 1996 pre-Open record included a victory in the Dubai Desert Classic and second-place finishes at the Deutsche Bank Open in Germany and the Alamo English Open.

Two other foreign golfers were getting strong mention, especially Singh from Fiji, a four-time winner on the PGA Tour who was hot during the first three months of 1996, finishing tied for eighth in the Hawaiian Open, tied for second behind Norman at the Doral-Ryder Open in Miami, tied for ninth behind Herron at the Honda Classic, tied for eighth when Couples won at The Players Championship and tied for fifth behind Loren Roberts at Hilton Head.

Els, winner of the 1994 U.S. Open at Oakmont, Pennsylvania, was having a mediocre PGA Tour season until late May when the 27-year-old flash from Johannesburg tied for sixth behind Watson at the Memorial and then, the weekend before Oakland Hills, won by eight strokes at Westchester with rounds of 65-66-69-71.

In addition, Ian Woosnam won the PGA European Tour's first two events of 1996, and Masashi (Jumbo) Ozaki arrived at Oakland Hills after again dominating the Japan PGA Tour with four early victories. The major champions of 1995 were also on hand: defending champion Corey Pavin, Ben Crenshaw (Masters), John Daly (British Open) and Steve Elkington (PGA Championship).

Sixty-nine golfers, including a majority of the sport's biggest names, had earned exemptions from qualifying for Oakland Hills. That left 87 spots in a 156-man Open field, made available to pros and amateurs with no worse than a 2.4 handicap index. The total number of entrants was 5,925.

From that ambitious army, 595 would advance from 80 courses where 18-hole local qualifiers were staged. Next stop would be 13 sectional qualifying sites and 36-hole grinds that would produce the 87 starters for Oakland Hills.

They all had dreams, to make it through all stages of U.S. Open qualifying, then to stun the world by winning the most difficult championship in golf, like Jack Fleck did in 1955 when he beat Ben Hogan in a championship playoff at San Francisco, or as Orville Moody accomplished in 1969 when the 33-year-old former army sergeant kept driving until he had won that Open in Houston.

As the 150 pros and six amateurs were grinding through final Open preparations, the Oakland Hills course was buried by a Wednesday rainstorm. More than two inches fell in a brief deluge. Bunkers were flooded. One fairway had a pond three feet deep.

Once the rain subsided, the grounds crew worked deep into the night to make the South Course playable on Thursday. Workers were brought in from several other Detroit area courses. Pumps were hooked up on several holes.

While forecasts were for more rain on Thursday, the skies would mercifully relent. Sunshine would appear late in the first round and dominate through the remainder of the weekend.

A rainstorm Wednesday afternoon washed out fairways and flooded bunkers, but the grounds crew worked into the night to repair the damage.

96th U.S. Open
First Round

Rain bombarded and puddled Oakland Hills on the eve of the U.S. Open's first round, taking a bit of the famous sting out of the par-70 South Course's greens but, conversely, making 6,974 yards play, when compared to a more customary par-72 standard, as though it was maybe 7,300 yards.

Payne Stewart, Open champion in 1991, would tie for Thursday's lead with one-time Florida bank teller Woody Austin at three-under-par 67. Twelve golfers broke par. One stroke off the lead at 68 were 1993 Open winner Lee Janzen and local longshot John Morse, the only Michigan native in the 156-man field.

"I played just about as perfectly as I'm capable of," said the 32-year-old Austin, the 1995 PGA Tour Golf Digest/Rolex Rookie of the Year. "I drove it pretty much where I wanted, got the ball into good position on the greens and even putted okay." Austin was the only golfer in the field to perform without a bogey, making three birdies and 15 pars.

Austin worked for years at a credit union in Tampa, even when playing mini tours in Florida, then graduated to the Nike Tour. "I was afraid to quit," Austin said. "Golf isn't exactly a steady job until you get a bunch in the bank."

In 1988, Austin laid off from golf almost 18 months to rehabilitate his left knee. Injured in a childhood baseball mishap, the knee failed to properly develop. During that period, Woody worked not only as a bank teller but as a graveyard-shift shelf stocker at a drug store.

"I think I've paid a few dues," said the slender pro who wears eyeglasses on the course. "My background is a bit different from many on the PGA Tour. I hope it makes me more appreciative of everything good that happens to me in golf. I've been living a dream for the 18 months coming to Oakland Hills."

Jack Nicklaus, playing in his 40th consecutive U.S. Open at 56, shot an unspectacular but most respectable two-over-par 72. No birdies, 16 pars, two bogeys. "I had a chance to get in position with the contenders," said the winner of four U.S. Opens and 16 other majors, "but I blew that chance."

Nicklaus was paired with the only other 50-and-over seniors in the field, his old Ohio State University associate Tom Weiskopf (53) and three-time Open champion Hale Irwin (51). Irwin shot 72 in the first round, Weiskopf 76.

"My time has probably passed," Nicklaus said, "but I'm going to go down fighting. I could well have shot 69 or 70. I was there, but I just didn't take advantage of my scoring opportunities."

Greg Norman suggested, two days before the Open began, that golf technology would ease the fabled toughness of Oakland Hills. But when the Shark teed off Thursday, after smacking a perfect drive on No. 1, he stumbled to a double-bogey six. Norman steadied, while fighting a virus, and shot 73. He was tied for 65th place.

Thursday's most-watched group featured 1995 U.S. Open winner Corey Pavin and two of the longest hitters in golf, reigning British Open champion John Daly and two-time U.S. Amateur winner Eldrick (Tiger) Woods.

None among the bombastic threesome

Payne Stewart, the 1991 champion, was four under par on the second nine for his 67 to share the first-round lead.

First Round

Lee Janzen, the 1993 champion, had six birdies and four bogeys in his 68.

Woody Austin shot 67 with no bogeys.

John Morse was the lone Michigan native.

had a sizzling round. Daly hit 14 of 18 greens in regulation but managed only a two-over-par 72. Pavin had 73. But it was 20-year-old Stanford University sophomore Woods who, for sweet and sour reasons, became the first round's spiciest story.

Woods was sensational for his first 13 holes, rising into a tie for the lead at three under par. He often outdrove Daly, hitting one gasping tee shot 340 yards. But there would come a humbling. Tiger suddenly lost his stripes. After being minus three, he went nine over par for the concluding five holes, including a quadruple-bogey eight at the 16th. Woods wound up tied for 115th place with a round of 76.

"It was a stretch of bad holes that I will never forget," said the lithe young talent, managing a smile. "But if you know and love golf, you understand how humbling it can be. If you don't accept that the wonderful highs will be balanced with some painful lows, well, this isn't the game for you. Life goes on. I'm eager for tomorrow."

Woods, who would appear to have a world of golden tomorrows, began to sink from atop Oakland Hills leaderboards with a bogey at the 14th hole, where he chipped poorly over a drain and then two-putted for bogey five. It was a preamble to deeper suffering.

At the 15th, the 155-pound Tiger drove into deep rough and would three-putt en route to double-bogey six. Woods was suddenly at even par. But the worst was lurking ahead on the 403-yard 16th.

His six-iron second shot faded, slipping right of the green and bouncing into a lake. Woods took a drop and looped a lob-wedge fourth shot onto the green, 10 feet from the cup. But it wouldn't stop there. Tiger's ball had such backspin that it drew down a slope, off the putting surface, down that same grassy slope and into the same water hazard. Woods would then plop his sixth shot onto the green. That time it stayed. He two-putted for the eight.

Tiger bogeyed the 17th. On the way to the 18th tee, a frustrated NCAA champion took a whack at a rake with his fickle putter. Then he also bogeyed the treacherous 465-

A large gallery saw Tiger Woods rise to the lead then tumble to 76.

First Round

Despite posting 69s, Paul Azinger (left) and Jumbo Ozaki had their patience tested in the afternoon play.

yard closing hole, a par-four that played as Oakland Hill's toughest (4.518 average) on Thursday.

But the maturation of Tiger Woods became more evident as the highly pressured young man talked philosophically about his rise and fall in the Open's first round. Pavin, a smallish grinder who has found PGA Tour greatness, saw Tiger qualities beyond the kid's thundering golf swing.

"I saw so many things to like during the 18 holes," the 36-year-old Pavin said of Woods. "His composure was excellent when Tiger got to three under, leading the U.S. Open, but then he also did pretty darn well in not erupting over that snowman (eight on the 16th) and the rest of his shaky finish.

"I know a lot of old pros who would've had steam coming from their collars and clubs flying from their bags. I see no reason why Tiger Woods won't become a great player. Man, can he smoke some shots. A little refinement on Tiger's short game and there'll be nothing. He's already pretty darn imposing."

First Round

Payne Stewart	67	-3
Woody Austin	67	-3
Lee Janzen	68	-2
John Morse	68	-2
David Berganio	69	-1
Bob Ford	69	-1
Philip Walton	69	-1
Gary Trivisonno	69	-1
Stewart Cink	69	-1
Frank Nobilo	69	-1
Masashi Ozaki	69	-1
Paul Azinger	69	-1

After leading the Open for 13 holes, Woods would finish Thursday in third place among six amateurs in the field. University of Florida sophomore Steve Scott, three weeks shy of his 19th birthday, was Thursday's best amateur with one-over 71, followed by Wendell (Jay) Hobby Jr., a rising senior from Auburn University who shot 74.

Ireland's Philip Walton was competing in his first U.S. Open Championship.

New Zealand's Frank Nobilo was disappointed with his first-round 69.

Stewart Cink was in the rough only two times in the first round while shooting his 69.

David Berganio won the 1991 and 1993 U.S. Amateur Public Links Championship.

First Round

Club professionals Bob Ford (left) and Gary Trivisonno were among the 12 contestants under par.

Two club professionals were among the dozen golfers breaking par in round one. Bob Ford and Gary Trivisonno had 69s. Ford, 42, has been head pro at Oakmont, site of six U.S. Opens, since 1980. Trivisonno, 39, is head pro at Aurora (Ohio) Country Club.

"I'm ecstatic simply to be a part of this Open field and to be playing well," said Ford, a former University of Tampa standout. "My first goal is to make the cut. If that happens, my goal becomes the top 15, so I'll be invited for the 1997 Open."

Trivisonno said he had been especially inspired by comments attributed to a PGA Tour regular, suggesting that club pros should be excluded from major championships. "That kind of gets your blood flowing when you hear something like that," said Trivisonno, who had played in four previous majors, but having not made the cuts in three PGA Championships and one U.S. Open.

"A lot of us club pros can play the game," said the one-time University of Alabama golfer. "Look at Tom Wargo and Jimmy Albus who went from club jobs to stardom on the Senior PGA Tour. I find it insulting to suggest that we simply be erased from the major championship picture."

Morse, a 38-year-old former University of Michigan golfer, was playing his fourth U.S. Open and in marvelous position to survive the 36-hole cut for the first time. His 32-36–68 was punctuated by holing out from a bunker to birdie the tough 18th, one of only seven threes accomplished on the climactic monster.

"I felt real good out there," said the PGA Tour regular born in Marshall, Michigan. "I hit a lot of three woods off tees, which tends to widen those narrow fairways." Morse's only PGA Tour win came in the 1995 United Airlines Hawaiian Open. His best pre-Open finish in 1996 was also in Hawaii, an eighth-place effort.

While the 18th was Thursday's most difficult hole, Oakland Hills' two par-fives were predictably the easiest, the 560-yard 12th playing at a scoring average of 4.690 and the 523-yard second falling at 4.774.

The average score for the entire field was 73.588, the back nine playing slightly tougher (36.972) than the front (36.616). Only the two par-five holes played under par.

96th U.S. Open

After his 72, Jack Nicklaus said, "I had seven or eight putts inside 15 feet and I didn't make any of them."

Payne Stewart left this shot in the bunker at No. 9 for a double bogey.

Defending champion Corey Pavin said Oakland Hills deserved its "monster" nickname.

96th U.S. Open
Second Round

Friday sunshine dried, hardened, quickened and restored the famous toughness of the Oakland Hills greens. Low scores continued to flow, but there came a predictable stabilizing and South Course leaderboards became stocked with more celebrities than surprises.

Twenty golfers shot in the 60s during the second round, compared to 12 on Thursday, but when 36 holes of varying artistry among the 156 starters was completed, there were just four red scoreboard totals glistening in the Michigan sunset.

Oakland Hills giveth, but it also taketh away. Not a single player had an under-par score both Thursday and Friday. Thirty-two sub-par rounds were shot the first two days, but just four players would wind up with under-par aggregates for 36 holes.

So tightly bunched was the field that a record 108 golfers survived the midway cut. Fifty-four were within six strokes of the lead. Saturday morning's headline on the *Detroit Free Press* sports section would scream: "Wide Open."

Payne Stewart, winner of the 1991 Open at Hazeltine in Minnesota, marginally slipped from an opening 67 to one-over-par 71, bogeying Friday's 16th and 18th holes, but the guy with the Ben Hogan cap and Gene Sarazen plus-four britches nonetheless had popped ahead by Oakland Hills' midway point.

Greg Norman, haunted by his 1996 Masters collapse plus the medical nag of a virus, used a warming putter as a U.S. Open joy stick in escalating from a Thursday 73 to a Friday 66. The Shark happily plunged from 35 putts to 28 and arose from a first-round tie for 65th place to a second-round runner-up deadlock with Woody Austin and Ernie Els, one stroke behind Stewart.

Norman finished his Friday round several hours ahead of Stewart. There was a stunning highlight as Greg's eight-iron approach to the 16th green hit six feet behind the cup and backspun somewhat sideways into the hole for an eagle two.

By the time Norman putted out on the 18th, his 66 vaulted the Australian into a tie for sixth place. But as Oakland Hills' greens became harder, faster and more spike-marked in the late afternoon, scoring got tougher. Norman's name kept rising on Open leaderboards until it would be higher or equal to all but one.

"I'm not out to prove anybody wrong," said Norman, who for the first time in years was not a popular media pick to win a major championship, surely due to his fourth-round collapse against Nick Faldo in the Masters. "This week is no different from last week on the Tour at Westchester," said an unsmiling Shark after his Friday upsurge at the Open. "No different than it'll be for me in a couple of weeks at Hartford."

Greg Norman scored an eagle two at the 16th hole (inset) and shot 66 to climb to a second-place tie behind Payne Stewart.

Second Round

Payne Stewart held a three-stroke lead before bogeys here at the 16th and then the 18th hole reduced his margin to one stroke and allowed 22 more contestants to survive the 36-hole cut.

Ernie Els saved par from a plugged lie at the 12th hole and finished with 67–139.

Norman said his second round at Oakland Hills was "pretty much a carbon copy of Thursday" except for improved putting. Statistics proved his point. Greg hit 12 of 14 fairways each day. He reached 14 of 18 greens in regulation during the first round, then 13 on Friday. But his putt total dropped by seven and so did his score.

The only others under par for 36 holes were Austin, the 1995 PGA Tour Golf Digest/Rolex Rookie of the Year with 67-72–139, and 1994 U.S. Open champion Ernie Els, the South African accomplishing the same scores but in reverse order.

Stewart would single-handedly create Saturday/Sunday jobs for 22 well-dressed golf workers. Everybody within 10 shots of the lead makes the U.S. Open cut. Payne was at four under par with three Friday holes to play. The best guess was that a six-over-par 146 total, assuming even-par scores on 16 through 18 by leader Stewart, would be the highest number to survive the 36-hole axe.

But then the 39-year-old pro from Or-

Frank Nobilo, hitting his second shot here into the No. 1 green, started the second round with two birdies and finished with a 71–140 total.

lando bogeyed the 16th, breathing extended Open life into 11 golfers who would have seven-over-par 147 totals. Stewart followed by bogeying the vicious 18th, allowing 11 more golfers at 148 to stick around Oakland Hills for the closing 36 holes.

But this Open's most astonishing second-round number of all was a bedazzling six-under-par 29 scored by Neal Lancaster on the fierce back nine. Only one other time in a U.S. Open, through all the gallant golfing eras of Bobby Jones and Ben Hogan and Jack Nicklaus and Hale Irwin, had a man achieved 29.

Guess who!

Same man.

In the 1995 Open at Shinnecock Hills on the eastern tip of Long Island, New York, this same uncelebrated 33-year-old pro had 29 for his concluding nine holes on Sunday. Lancaster came out of New York obscurity with his 36-29–65 to finish fourth behind champion Corey Pavin.

Even so, in Lancaster's pre-U.S. Open tournaments on the 1996 PGA Tour, he had

Neal Lancaster's 29 matched his own U.S. Open record for nine holes.

Second Round

First off on Thursday, Ken Green drew more notice on Friday with his 67 and his putter.

USGA officials monitored the pace of play.

Second Round

Payne Stewart	67 - 71 – 138	-2
Greg Norman	73 - 66 – 139	-1
Ernie Els	72 - 67 – 139	-1
Woody Austin	67 - 72 – 139	-1
Davis Love III	71 - 69 – 140	E
Frank Nobilo	69 - 71 – 140	E
Ken Green	73 - 67 – 140	E
Sam Torrance	71 - 69 – 140	E
Steve Jones	74 - 66 – 140	E

European star Sam Torrance was among those at even par for 36 holes.

managed to finish in the top 30 only three times in 18 chances. That 29 at Shinnecock Hills seemed a fluke. Lancaster's first-round result at Oakland Hills was an unimposing 37-37–74, tying him for 84th place.

After Friday's front nine, making the Open cut seemed little more than a Lancaster semi-fantasy. He had struggled to a three-over-par 38. By then, Neal was buried in 110th place. During his first 27 holes at Oakland Hills, the fellow from Smithfield, North Carolina, had just two birdies while suffering seven bogeys and a double bogey.

Lancaster merely parred the 10th hole, but then he birdied the 11th. Then came an eagle three on the 560-yard 12th. Lancaster was into a remarkable five-hole eruption. He also birdied the 13th and 14th and 15th. From there, Neal parred his way home. Another 29. Another miracle by a golfer

Davis Love III said he avoided trouble but had few opportunities for birdies.

Tiger Woods shot 69 with three three-putt greens, having four bogeys and five birdies.

who had been a stranger to big-time golf headlines, having won just one tournament in seven PGA Tour years.

Even his lone Tour trophy came in weird fashion. Dallas-Fort Worth had been flogged by constant rain during the 1994 GTE Byron Nelson Classic. Sponsors decided to reduce the tournament to a rare 36-hole competition. Lancaster and five other golfers wound up tied with rather exceptional 132 totals. Neal then won the half-a-tournament in a playoff.

At mid-round on Friday at Oakland Hills, both Lancaster and his family supporters had pretty much given up on making the Open cut. His father, Charles, and a couple of buddies had driven the Lancaster family van from North Carolina to Michigan to see Neal's performance in the 96th Open. But after the non-competitive 74 of Thursday, the van made an early Friday getaway back toward Smithfield.

Tom Kite rebounded with a 76-71–147 total.

Second Round

As usual, Scott Simpson was contending with a 141 total, including 71 in the second round.

Senior Open champion Tom Weiskopf missed the 36-hole cut with a 76-75–151 total.

Senior Tour regular Hale Irwin was well placed at 143 after rounds of 72 and 71.

Even Lancaster said to himself after his front-nine 38, "Let's get it over with." The van was long gone. Charles and company were on a southbound highway somewhere in southern Ohio when Neal suddenly flowered with another Open 29. "Maybe they're spending Friday night at some motel about 400 miles away," Lancaster would say. "I hope they don't decide to turn around and come back. They're bad luck." He said it with a grin. Neal's 38-29–67 bounced him up to a 10th-place tie after two days.

Sixteen times in Open history, golfers from Jim McHale in 1947 to Els in 1994 had scores of 30 for nine holes. Among them were Arnold Palmer, Ken Venturi, Bob Charles, Raymond Floyd, Chip Beck, Paul Azinger, Scott Simpson and Peter Jacobsen. But nobody had ever done it twice.

Thirty seemed the unpenetrable barrier, until Lancaster came along most unpredictably at Shinnecock Hills, then did it again against monumental odds at Oakland Hills.

The lowest 18-hole score ever in a U.S. Open was 63, accomplished by Johnny Miller in the final round of his 1973 championship at Oakmont and then equalled by both Tom Weiskopf and eventual winner Jack Nicklaus at Baltusrol in 1980.

Among the second-round bounce-backs among Oakland Hills contenders, the 66s by Norman and Steve Jones were most imposing, along with the Lancaster doozie. Jones, who had bogeys on three par-three holes in his opening 74, made birdies on three of his first six holes in the second round. After one bogey, he scored birdies on the par-five 12th hole and par-three 13th, then posted pars on the five tough finishing holes.

Two-time U.S. Amateur champion Tiger Woods also brilliantly rallied from his tribulations of a Thursday 76 by shooting one-under-par 69. Tiger's turnaround was especially evident on the South Course's rigorous five finishing holes, a stretch that had given Woods a nine-over-par Thursday beating including his twice-watered, quadruple-bogey eight at the 16th. Friday's story became a two-under-par success for the finishing five holes, an 11-stroke flopflip. This time he birdied the par-four 16th, an improvement of five blows on that hole alone.

For a second consecutive round, the 465-yard 18th played harder than any hole, the par-four averaging 4.549 strokes. Also among the tough exam of those five closing holes were the second toughest, par-four No. 14 (4.392), and also the South Course's eighth most difficult, the par-three 17th (3.235).

While the second 29 in an U.S. Open by Lancaster was the most longshot occurrence among the 156 golfers, an even more against-the-odds happening involved an Oakland Hills spectator named Chuck McDonald. The 51-year-old man from Willis, Michigan, made an early Friday decision that the 16th hole, which had been such a Tiger Woods tormentor in the opening round, was a supreme spot from which to observe the second round going on.

A doubly painful decision.

This unlucky spectator was hit twice at the 16th hole by errant golf shots.

In the morning, Steve Lowery hit an approach shot that took a bounce and glanced off McDonald's head. It was a bit painful, but the Open customer shook it off. He would have a U.S. Open war wound to show the folks at work come Monday morning.

But then, perhaps setting some sort of major championship record, McDonald would get hit again. This time by a golf ball off the club of the tournament leader.

Stewart approached the 16th with a three-stroke advantage over runners-up Els, Norman and Austin. Payne, creating a kind of sporting pain for himself, pulled his iron shot left of the green that would lead to a bogey five. But the errant Stewart missile would also plunk McDonald, this one cracking against his head on the fly. It really hurt. McDonald bled. He was taken to a hospital, then released with a bandage. "I don't think," the spectator said, "I'll be going back to the 16th hole any more."

96th U.S. Open
Third Round

All around the world, on the most prominent of golfing stages, the third round is considered "Moving Day." Saturday's 18 holes are a critical, adjusting time in which pretenders often fade and contenders are expected to jockey for healthy positions in Sunday's sprint to the finish.

Tom Lehman, never a winner of a major but a powerful player who finished third in both the 1993 Masters and the 1995 U.S. Open, took an early fast lane to Saturday prominence at Oakland Hills.

Finishing two hours ahead of other leaderboard occupants, the 37-year-old Lehman had charmed the "Frightful Five" finishing holes with birdie brilliance, allowing him to tie the course record with 32-33–65.

"At the time, with so many players still on the course," Lehman would say, "my biggest motivation in grinding out a par on the final hole was to tie that record. I really like the sound of my name being grouped with those who have shot the best round ever at a course as difficult as Oakland Hills."

Lehman was the eighth man to accomplish 65 on the South Course, the most recent among the others being Jack Nicklaus in the 1991 U.S. Senior Open.

At the 465-yard 18th, Lehman executed a spread-eagle bunker shot, left foot in the sand and his right propped on a grassy knoll. A preamble to a wonderful blast to within eight feet of the cup. Tom saved par, which would make a huge difference by day's end.

Lehman then hung around, doing interviews and greeting well-wishers while enjoying lunch, watching through the remainder of the sunny afternoon as his name took a steady upward flight among the Open hopefuls.

As forthcoming players became more and more wilt-prone, Tom's name never quit escalating until, at Saturday twilight, there were none above him. Lehman was the Open's 54-hole leader by one stroke with rounds of 71-72-65. Lehman jumped from 27th place to first on moving day.

Steve Jones, a comeback story after missing three PGA Tour years with a finger injury, made one of only four third-round birdies at the 18th to shoot 69 and join Lehman as the only golfers under par after 54 holes. Winless since 1989, when Jones took three Tour trophies, his numbers going into Sunday at Oakland Hills were 74-66-69.

Upstairs/downstairs movement was predictably considerable during the penultimate round on the 1996 Open schedule, but as golfers continually groped and winced through the South Course's salty finishing holes, some of Saturday's more stunning fallbacks would be by fellows who have known major championship success.

Ernie Els, 1994 U.S. Open winner at Oakmont, was atop Oakland Hills' leaderboards with four holes to go. Then the South African bogeyed the par-four 15th. That was bad, but his 16th hole was worse. Els pulled his tee shot into trees left of the fairway. "Go for it" was on his mind.

"I had a good lie, 160 yards from the green," he would say. "Seven iron seemed a reasonable choice. Only I didn't see that little limb that was hanging over me." Ernie ticked the tree on his takeaway, then rushed

Tom Lehman acknowledged the cheers after his 65 to equal the Oakland Hills record.

Third Round

A poor approach shot led to a bogey at the 18th as Ernie Els dropped four strokes on the last four holes.

"On 16, I did a little bit of everything," Payne Stewart said. "Amateurs would be proud of me."

his swing. His ball skidded onto rocks beside the pond at the 16th. Els took an unplayable drop and made double-bogey six. He finished two-over-par 72, three off the lead and tied for sixth place.

Payne Stewart, champion of the 1991 U.S. Open, pranced to a two-stroke lead until The Monster ate him. Stewart played the final seven holes in a shivering six over par. That sneaky mean 16th hole was also his Waterloo.

Payne's name might've immediately been respelled P-a-i-n. His drive at the 16th plunged into deep, menacing rough. Stewart made a questionable judgment. Instead of laying up from the cabbage stew, he attempted to flail a heroic shot to the green. It had no chance. Stewart semi-shanked his ball into the middle of what became known as "Tiger Woods Lake."

Steve Jones (opposite) had three birdies, including one of only four on No. 18 in the third round.

Third Round

Greg Norman's frustration was evident as he fell to a 15th-place tie at 74–213.

Third Round

Tom Lehman	71 - 72 - 65 – 208	-2
Steve Jones	74 - 66 - 69 – 209	-1
John Morse	68 - 74 - 68 – 210	E
Frank Nobilo	69 - 71 - 70 – 210	E
Davis Love III	71 - 69 - 70 – 210	E
Colin Montgomerie	70 - 72 - 69 – 211	+1
Jim Furyk	72 - 69 - 70 – 211	+1
Sam Torrance	71 - 69 - 71 – 211	+1
Woody Austin	67 - 72 - 72 – 211	+1
Ernie Els	72 - 67 - 72 – 211	+1

Stewart's trials were not over. After a drop, his fourth shot spun back off the green, managing to elude that same water only due to hanging up on a wad of grass. Payne then made a mediocre chip and two-putted for a triple-bogey seven. Stewart also bogeyed the par-three 17th, finishing with a round of 76. In a few miserable minutes,

Davis Love III drove the ball fairly well and made four birdies in his even-par round.

John Morse continued to challenge with his 68 that included five birdies over eight holes.

he had slipped from first place in the U.S. Open to a tie for 22nd.

Among the top-10 scorers for three rounds, only Els had won a major championship. Davis Love III, despite winning more than $5 million on the PGA Tour by age 30, had carried an enormous burden through much of his career. Until 1995, he had never finished in the top 10 in a major. Love broke through by winding up second to Ben Crenshaw in the 1995 Masters, then he was tied for fourth in the U.S. Open at Shinnecock Hills.

Now the North Carolinian was in strong shape again after 54 holes. For three days, Love had been the only golfer to play the five finishing holes under par. He was minus one. Lehman, the tournament leader, was even par on holes 14 through 18. Els, in aching comparison, was five over par.

"My goal was to be at even par after 54 holes," Love said, "and here I am. Still in the hunt. There's no question that the more you contended in a major, the more you mature." At age 32, the affable Love was talking with more hope than ever.

Saturday seemed such a perfect golfing day. Eighty degrees, little wind, voluminous sunshine. But, for many, there would be deep teeth marks from The Monster. One of the most grimacing of faces belonged to Greg Norman, who had vaulted into contention with his 66 on Friday.

There would be no Saturday firing pin on the Norman cannon. After 12 holes, the game's dominant personality had zero birdies and three bogeys. He was backsliding out of the Open spotlight. The Shark then birdied the 13th, but bogeyed the 14th. Coming to the fickle 16th, where Norman had holed an eight iron for eagle two on Friday, he was desperate for an uptick.

Norman's approach was sensational, 10 feet behind the cup. But his birdie putt slith-

Third Round

Colin Montgomerie led the statistics for hitting fairways and greens.

Frank Nobilo was proving himself well-suited to U.S. Open conditions.

ered past. He had pretty much the same deal on the par-three 17th. A good birdie chance. Another near-miss. But this time the Norman anger was more apparent. He would hit a 16-inch second putt that never grazed the hole. It was a three-putt bogey that socked Norman with a 74 and spiraled the famous thunder from Down Under into a tie for 15th place. So flustered was the Shark after his 16-inch miscue that Norman soon was turning to ask Stewart, his similarly agonized companion, "What did I make on that hole?"

After handling his Sunday flameout at the Masters with patience, grace and even smiles, a stern-faced Norman refused any media discussions after Saturday's disappointment at this U.S. Open. Stewart, meanwhile, dealt with his back-nine traumas with remarkable calm and even humor.

Sam Torrance putted well to be within three strokes of the lead at 71–211.

Tom Watson, with 71, had "an up and down round," finishing at 212.

Woody Austin said that balls were bouncing on bumpy greens late in the day.

"My mess started when I fatted a sand wedge shot at the 12th and made bogey six," said the former SMU golfer. "I hit a perfect tee shot at the 15th but missed the green with a seven iron. Then came that 16th. Oh, baby, that one goes down in history. I did what every amateur golfer sees in nightmares.

"I shank one out of the rough and into the middle of the water. Looking very much like a 20-handicapper. Then a fat wedge. On and on until I get a triple bogey. I just had to smile. It seemed to be a better option than seeing a grown man cry before millions of people."

After the movements of Saturday, those nearest to sub-par golfers Lehman and Jones, sitting two strokes off the lead, were Love, Frank Nobilo and John Morse at even-par 210. Woody Austin, a contender for 36 holes, shot 72 to drop into a sixth-place tie at 211 with Els, Colin Montgomerie, Sam Torrance and Jim Furyk.

"It's so tightly bunched going into Sunday," said Tom Watson, winner of the 1982 U.S. Open and seven other major championships, "that anybody within five or six of the lead can explode into contention with a round that approaches that 65 shot by Lehman."

Watson was four behind Lehman at two-over-par 212 along with John Cook, Ken Green and 23-year-old Stewart Cink out of Georgia Tech. Three dozen players were within seven of the lead when the combatants showed up for the fourth round.

While many of golf's bigger celebrities were tumbling down flights of Oakland Hills stairs, one of the more hurrahed figures on moving day was Morse. The local guy. Michigan's lone local golfer in this Open, he had retrogressed after a stunning Thursday 68, shooting 74 in the second round. But then, instead of continuing a slide, Morse would be reborn as a challenger. He carved out another 68 on Saturday and entered the concluding 18 holes trailing nobody but Lehman and Jones.

Morse was asked about his sudden celebrity, doing interviews before 300 reporters in the Open media tent and being featured on ESPN, NBC, CNN and every Detroit television station. "Paparazzi," the 38-year-old pro said, "that is part of the deal. I have had good experiences with TV in countries other than the United States. I have media experience. It's not being thrust on me. It's no big deal."

Nobilo, locked with Morse and Love at 210, showed considerably more flair. His great-grandfather was an Italian pirate who settled in Frank's homeland of New Zealand. "I thought Shinnecock was the best, toughest golf course I'd ever played on (in the 1995 U.S. Open), but this place (Oakland Hills) is unbelievable. It is certainly not unfair, but it's really tough. A wonderful championship venue."

At 36, Nobilo was continuing to amass a strong reputation for competing on U.S. Open courses. In his first chance at Oakmont in 1994, the Kiwi tied for ninth behind champion Els with even-par 284. At Shinnecock Hills, he tied for 10th when Corey Pavin won, shooting five-over 285.

Jim Furyk was three strokes off the lead after bogeying three of the last five holes.

96th U.S. Open

Fourth Round

Down the stretch the U.S. Open horses came. Tom Lehman and Davis Love III were predictable challengers. Prodigious talents from America's professional golf tour. Rich, famous men with considerable expectations, aiming to crack through and embrace a first major championship.

Plus a fellow named Steve Jones.

John Morse, a homegrown Michigan hope, was gallantly hanging on. Then, one last time, the 38-year-old global golf journeyman came to the finishing holes. He wobbled with a bogey at the pivotal 16th, then would surrender from trophy possibilities by bogeying the long and crusty 18th. Morse finished fourth at even-par 280.

As the 96th Open neared a testy but enthralling Sunday conclusion on Oakland Hills' excruciating back nine, the competitive fires of some of golf's most recognizable heroes — Jack Nicklaus, Greg Norman, Curtis Strange, Ernie Els, Nick Faldo and defending champion Corey Pavin — were either doused or severely flickering.

At the most climactic of moments, the biggest of guns would not be factors for the biggest of golf prizes. Faldo, winner of the 1996 Masters, never got his Open bid in racing gear, finishing tied for 16th with five-over-par 285.

Nicklaus, however, was hailed all through the warm Sunday, as though the

Ernie Els shot even-par 70 and shared fifth place with Jim Furyk at 281.

Jack Nicklaus completed his 40th consecutive U.S. Open.

Golden Bear were winning a fifth U.S. Open and 21st major championship. In his 40th consecutive Open and 138th major in a row, the 56-year-old golfing colossus was cheered by standing throngs at every tee, along all Oakland Hills fairways and especially around greens during what could be his last truly competitive U.S. Open moment.

"When I finished the 1995 Open with an 81 at Shinnecock Hills," Nicklaus would say, "I ran into (USGA President) Judy Bell and told her I didn't want an 81 to be my last Open score. I was graciously granted a special invitation. I've played not so badly. But I want no more such invitations.

"If I come back, I want to earn it, like perhaps by winning in the U.S. Senior Open. Except, of course, perhaps years from now, when I might come to the Open one more time just to say goodbye." Nicklaus shot 72-74-69-72–287 at Oakland Hills, tying him for 27th place.

The stage was clearing.

Golfers who had been Open leaders earlier in the weekend were by late Sunday spiraling deep into the pack. Kiwi favorite Frank Nobilo played his final five holes in five over par, plunging to a tie for 13th place.

Woody Austin, a contender going into the last nine, stumbled to two double bogeys and a six-over-par 41 to fall to a tie for 23rd. Payne Stewart, the Open leader after 50 holes, wound up tied for 27th.

Fourth Round

Greg Norman did not challenge on the last day, and tied for 10th place at 283.

A final-round 72 left Colin Montgomerie five strokes behind at 283.

Dan Forsman shot 71–284 and tied for 13th place, six strokes behind.

Norman, twice champion of British Opens, continued to come short of a major championship on his adopted American soil. His near-misses had become legend, but this time Greg wasn't close at the trophy hour. He tied for 10th place at three-over-par 283.

In a 15-year run, the Shark had three second-place windups in the Masters, including his ghastly 78 in the final 1996 round to toss the tournament to Faldo. He had also been third twice, fourth once, fifth once and sixth once at Augusta.

U.S. Opens had brought Norman two seconds, a fifth and a sixth. In PGA Championships, he had been second twice, fourth twice, and fifth. In all, 17 top-six finishes in American majors without winning one.

"I've got nothing to prove to anybody," Norman said. "Every time, I try my hardest to win. Can anybody ask more? I've had my chances. I will keep trying. I'm a winner, I know that."

The 1996 Open would eventually come down to three horses. After 71 holes, the triumvirate of Lehman, Love and a PGA Tour comeback wonder named Jones represented all the remaining thoroughbreds with chances to win. With the teeth-gnashing, gut-wrenching, 465-yard 18th left to negotiate, each man stood at two under par for the week.

Love was first to finish. It was Father's Day and Davis III bubbled with desire to win this monumental championship, to be dedicated to his late father, one of the world's more renowned teaching pros before dying in an airplane crash.

Love's critical examination would be a slick, downhill, 15-foot birdie putt. If he could slither it into the cup, the Open would probably belong to the kid with the high pockets out of the University of North Carolina. A two-putt was likely to qualify Davis for a Monday 18-hole playoff with Jones, Lehman or both.

That 15-footer turned out to be shy on boldness, slipping down that slope but stopping three feet shy of the cup. Love then missed that one, socking himself with bogey five.

For the ensuing 15 minutes, Love would sit beside that green with 20,000 others. Checking out the competition. Seeing what the final Open group of Lehman and Jones would do. Knowing he had probably squashed a dream with that three-putt.

Out in the fairway, Lehman got unlucky. His tee shot appeared to be a gem, but the ball took a nasty bounce into a bunker, leaving the powerful fellow from Minnesota no chance to go for the green in two. Meanwhile, the unflappable 6-foot-4 Jones, an Open longshot of indecipherable proportions, nailed his tee ball into the heart of the good, short grass.

Lehman pitched out of that bunker, wedged onto the green and had a 15-footer for par. Jones then struck an extraordinary, high-pressure, seven-iron approach from 170 yards, bouncing it once at the front of the green and then for a heart-fluttering second time within an inch of the cup. A near Open-winning hole-out for eagle two.

Ken Green's 70 earned a share of seventh place, four strokes behind at 282.

Frank Nobilo shot 74, dropping five strokes on the last five holes, for a 284 total.

Fourth Round

Jim Furyk's 70 provided a top-five placing.

Vijay Singh shot 69 for a seventh-place tie.

But, instead, the Jones golf ball wound up 14 feet behind the hole, just inside of Lehman's.

Lehman snaked his par putt wide left. Bogey five. A tie at one-under-par 279 with Love. Clearing the stage for a champion. Love was biting his lip, taking deep breaths and wishing he could have a do-over of his shortfalling first putt on that 18th green. Davis instead could only watch Jones, along with all the world, as Steve deftly nuzzled a speedy first putt to within 18 inches of the hole. Then he tapped in, becoming a most unlikely U.S. Open winner.

"This is the thrill of a lifetime," Jones would say. "Every young boy who plays golf grows up dreaming about having a putt to win the U.S. Open. Lucky for me, it was a 18-incher. My gut was wrenching, my heart pounding and my head spinning. Thank God for the opportunity. Thank God for everything."

Love had become a latter-day major challenger. After not finishing in the top 10 of

Fourth Round

Steve Jones	74 -66 -69 -69 – 278	-2
Davis Love III	71 -69 -70 -69 – 279	-1
Tom Lehman	71 -72 -65 -71 – 279	-1
John Morse	68 -74 -68 -70 – 280	E
Ernie Els	72 -67 -72 -70 – 281	+1
Jim Furyk	72 -69 -70 -70 – 281	+1
Scott Hoch	73 -71 -71 -67 – 282	+2
Vijay Singh	71 -72 -70 -69 – 282	+2
Ken Green	73 -67 -72 -70 – 282	+2
Lee Janzen	68 -75 -71 -69 – 283	+3
Greg Norman	73 -66 -74 -70 – 283	+3
Colin Montgomerie	70 -72 -69 -72 – 283	+3

Not the most famous of contenders, Steve Jones (opposite) established his credentials as the U.S. Open champion.

Tom Lehman's drive at the 18th took a hard bounce left into a bunker, leaving him no chance to reach the green in two and resulting in a bogey to tie for second place.

any major championship until 1995, when he was Masters runner-up and then finished fourth behind Pavin in the U.S. Open.

"I'm a little bit closer," he said after the near-miss at Oakland Hills, "but a lot more disappointed." Love recalled a 1987 moment when, at the Heritage Classic on Hilton Head Island, South Carolina, he won for the first time on the PGA Tour due to a 72nd-hole misfire by rising young pro Steve Jones.

"Steve was going to win until he drove it out of bounds on the final hole," Love recalled. "He basically gave me my first Tour win. I guess this is payback, me three-putting the 72nd hole in the Open to open the door for Steve. But somehow I don't feel as though I've broken even."

After his golden little putt, Jones was cheered as the ultimate underdog who had won the most expansive of golfing glories. Two little Jones children, Cy and Stacey, leaped into the champion's arms on Father's

After a shocking three-putt bogey at the 18th, Davis Love III (opposite) was left to watch the final two groups, knowing he had probably squashed his dream.

John Morse bogeyed the 16th and 18th holes, finishing two strokes behind.

Fourth Round

After driving into the middle of the fairway, Steve Jones hit the seven-iron shot of his life, nearly holing out from 170 yards, then two-putted for a par to win the championship.

Jones and Lehman embraced at the finish.

Day. After loads of pain, Steve Jones was feeling nothing but good.

Jones has come back from a injury that robbed him of three prime-of-career years. His left ring finger was dislocated in a dirt-biking wreck. Steve kept trying to return to golf and reinjuring the finger.

At 32, he had won four PGA Tour events and earned more than $2 million. But that bummed-up finger would idle Jones through all of 1992 and 1993 plus most of 1994. His return, for 18 months, had been steadily upbeat but with neither victory nor heavy public/media attention.

Until now, at age 37, with Jones demolishing all the favorites at Oakland Hills, beginning with a lukewarm and unnoticed 74 before going into a remarkable 66-69-69–204 run (one stroke off the Open record for the final 54 holes) for a two-under-par 278 that outdid Love, Lehman and all the rest.

"To come back from an injury that wiped Steve out for so long, then to win the Open, that is a remarkable story," said a dejected but stylish Lehman, who at 37 was a $4 mil-

Throughout the four days of competition at Oakland Hills, large galleries enjoyed beautiful weather and outstanding golf in the U.S. Open Championship.

lion achiever still yet to win a major championship. "I felt like I played well enough to win. You keep hearing, 'Your time will come,' but you come close and it gets frustrating."

Lehman began coming close by finishing in a tie for sixth in the 1992 U.S. Open. He tied for third in the 1993 Masters, was second at Augusta National in 1994, third at the 1995 U.S. Open and now tied for second at Oakland Hills.

Among four amateurs who made the 36-hole cut, the low finisher would not be celebrated two-time U.S. Amateur champion Tiger Woods. He shot a closing 72 for a 14-over-par 294 total. The Stanford sophomore was third among non-professionals.

Randy Leen, a college golfer from Indiana University, was low amateur at 291 after getting into the Open field as an alternate due to the medical withdrawals of Nick Price and Fred Couples. Trip Kuehne of Oklahoma State was second-low amateur at Oakland Hills with 293. Then came Woods at 294, and 18-year-old University of Florida sophomore Steve Scott at 301.

Randy Leen (left) received the low amateur medal from USGA President Judy Bell.

96th U.S. Open
The Champion

Steve Jones did it by the books. A religious man, he was a daily quoter of the Bible, a Christian who worked hard at walking in godly footsteps. But in the days before Steve flew to Detroit to play the United States Open, an Arizona neighbor put another book in Jones' hands that had undergone healing.

Hogan was a new Curt Sampson biography about one of golf's more dynamic, more inspirational, more successful practitioners, Ben Hogan, who ironically won the 1951 U.S. Open on the same famous Oakland Hills grass that Jones was about to challenge.

"While taking a week off in Montana, I couldn't put the book down," Steve would say in the afterglow of his own Open conquest on the South Course, which ranked as far more of a stunner than Hogan's. "Mr. Hogan's book contained such guidance in approaching this difficult game we try so hard to play. I don't think I would've won this Open if I hadn't read *Hogan*. What a mind, what determination and what powerful thoughts the great Ben has had about golf and about life."

Jones' opening Open round was an unspectacular 74. Four bogeys, no birdies. But then the mind, the mechanics and the production fell into sensational order. Steve shot 66 the second day with five birdies and one bogey. Then 69 on the third; three birdies, two bogeys including the 18th hole which 24 hours later would become such a memorable place in Jones' life. Even after Saturday's solid performance, there was little attention paid to Jones by Open media or the huge crowds around the South Course.

"I was grinding in the stomach," he recalled. "Incredibly nervous but also really excited and hopeful heading into Sunday. My game was feeling really good." Jones was about to become the first Open sectional qualifier since Jerry Pate in 1976 to win the championship.

When the show was finally over on Sunday, the longshot comeback guy had slicked his way to another 69 and a 204 score for the final 54 holes, one stroke off the all-time Open low accomplished by Loren Roberts at Oakmont in 1994.

In the climactic fourth round, Jones parred the first eight holes and then made birdie two at the ninth. On the fearsome back nine, he birdied the par-four 10th and the par-five 12th, but then bogeyed a pair of par-threes, the 13th and 17th, to set up the dramatics on the 18th.

During the final round, Lehman was an inspiration to Jones. A fellow Christian, he was quoting scripture. Most prominent of the message was, "The Lord wants us to be courageous and strong."

Hogan was another factor.

Ben came back from a devastating, life-threatening 1949 accident, when his car crashed head on into a bus on a Texas highway. His return was fully christened in 1951 when the wiry, iron-willed Texan won that Open at Oakland Hills.

Jones could identify.

Steve kept making it clear that he in no way was claiming to compare to Hogan. "Who can?" he remarked. "There will be only one Jack Nicklaus, one Arnold Palmer and only one Ben Hogan."

But the handsome young man from Colo-

Inspired by Hogan, *Steve Jones joined Ben as a champion at Oakland Hills.*

The Champion

"It's incredible," Jones said moments after his victory. "It's a thrill of a lifetime. Not in my wildest dreams would I have been able to believe this."

rado did nonetheless evolve into a productive player on the PGA Tour in the 1980s. He won the 1988 AT&T Pebble Beach National Pro-Am on the Pebble Beach links where major championships are often contested. Then, in 1989, Jones finished first three times, including back-to-back victories in the MONY Tournament of Champions and Bob Hope Desert Classic, and another win later that season in the Canadian Open.

By 1991, Jones had earned more than $2 million and was steaming into his golfing prime. His career was going nicely. Jones took some time off to relax. In November 1991, he went into the Arizona desert not far from his Scottsdale home to ride a dirt bike. It would be fateful. Painful. Career threatening. Not anywhere close to being as crushing at the Hogan bus accident two generations before, but nonetheless traumatic for Steve Jones.

"I was riding my dirt bike with a friend," Jones recalled. "He wrecked in front of me. I made a radical turn to avoid hitting him. I went flying. Got clobbered. Sprained an ankle. Separated my left shoulder. Also a little problem with the ring finger on my left hand, which would become the biggest difficulty of all."

Left hands are vital to righthanded golfers. It's their grip. Their control of clubs. To pros, their livelihood. Jones would appear to be healed, but then he would swing a golf club and reinjure the finger. Doctors were befuddled. It kept happening, costing Steve the entire 1992 season on the PGA Tour, then all of 1993, plus most of 1994.

Finally, in 1995, the finger got well. "I was still afraid to practice as much as a touring pro needs," he said. Paul Purtzer, older brother of PGA Tour veteran Tom Purtzer, had taken on Jones as a rehab project. An accomplished Arizona golf teacher, Paul tirelessly labored to recreate the abilities that Steve had enjoyed before the dirt bike crackup. Jones was making zero income at the time. Purtzer gave his lessons for free.

He developed a reverse overlapping grip to compensate for the sore finger. Good scores and high earnings began to return in 1995. Jones finished fourth at Phoenix and fifth in Memphis. In 1989, he had ranked eighth in Tour income. Steve rebounded to $234,749, ranking him 79th in 1995.

Celebrating the U.S. Open Championship with Jones were (from left) son Cy, wife Bonnie and daughter Stacey.

Improvement continued under Purtzer's eye in 1996, but few things in early 1996 would've suggested that Jones was about to win the U.S. Open on the punishing track at Oakland Hills. He did tie for 10th in his home-area PGA Tour stop at Phoenix, then tied for ninth at the Bay Hill Invitational in Orlando.

Then, in his six tournaments prior to the Open, the 37-year-old Jones would miss four cuts. His last tournaments before Oakland Hills were cut-missers at the Kemper Open and Memorial. During the stretch, Steve also tied for 51st in Dallas, but then would show flashes of old-time excellence, achieving a sixth-place tie in May at the MasterCard Colonial in Fort Worth.

Then came the book *Hogan*. Plus a lot of huddling with his Bible. On to Oakland Hills where the Jones career would take a demonstrative, indelible turn.

Jones was born in Artesia, New Mexico, but grew up in tiny Yuma, Colorado, where his dad introduced Steve to golf when the gangly kid was 12. "I was twice Colorado State Sand Greens champion," he says with both pride and a smile, referring to a grittier form of golf. Steve played golf, ran track and was all-state in basketball as a high school athlete, but he advanced to the University of Colorado and concentrated on golf.

In 1976, at age 17, Jones lost to eventual champion Madden Hatcher, 5 and 4, in the semifinals of the U.S. Junior Amateur at Evergreen, Colorado. Then, after his game matured in college, Steve turned pro in 1981 at 22.

Oh, did he forever give up dirt bikes after struggling with the fickle finger of fate for so long? Well, not immediately. "A couple of years later," Jones said, "I was trying to tune up the old bike and take it for a ride. I was going maybe five miles an hour and managed to flip the bike in a cul-de-sac near our house. That's when I said 'Enough!' No more bikes, but I do like riding wave-runners."

Any man who can win an Open by conquering, or at least surviving, the final five holes at Oakland Hills does merit the stamp of "adventurer." Hogan was an adventuresome, creative champion in 1951. Jones was the same in 1996. In some ways, comparing Ben and Steve is ludicrous. But not in all ways.

96th U.S. Open

June 13-16, 1996, Oakland Hills Country Club, Birmingham, Michigan

Contestant	Rounds				Total	Prize
Steve Jones	74	66	69	69	278	$425,000.00
Davis Love III	71	69	70	69	279	204,801.00
Tom Lehman	71	72	65	71	279	204,801.00
John Morse	68	74	68	70	280	111,235.00
Ernie Els	72	67	72	70	281	84,964.50
Jim Furyk	72	69	70	70	281	84,964.50
Scott Hoch	73	71	71	67	282	66,294.67
Vijay Singh	71	72	70	69	282	66,294.67
Ken Green	73	67	72	70	282	66,294.67
Lee Janzen	68	75	71	69	283	52,591.00
Greg Norman	73	66	74	70	283	52,591.00
Colin Montgomerie	70	72	69	72	283	52,591.00
Dan Forsman	72	71	70	71	284	43,725.33
Tom Watson	70	71	71	72	284	43,725.33
Frank Nobilo	69	71	70	74	284	43,725.33
Nick Faldo	72	71	72	70	285	33,188.29
David Berganio	69	72	72	72	285	33,188.29
Mark Brooks	76	68	69	72	285	33,188.29
Mark O'Meara	72	73	68	72	285	33,188.29
John Cook	70	71	71	73	285	33,188.29
Stewart Cink	69	73	70	73	285	33,188.29
Sam Torrance	71	69	71	74	285	33,188.29
Brad Bryant	73	71	74	68	286	23,806.00
Peter Jacobsen	71	74	70	71	286	23,806.00
Billy Andrade	72	69	72	73	286	23,806.00
Woody Austin	67	72	72	75	286	23,806.00
Curtis Strange	74	73	71	69	287	17,809.40
Peter Jordan	71	74	72	70	287	17,809.40
Jack Nicklaus	72	74	69	72	287	17,809.40
Payne Stewart	67	71	76	73	287	17,809.40
John Daly	72	69	73	73	287	17,809.40
Mike Swartz	72	72	74	70	288	14,070.50
Tom Purtzer	76	71	71	70	288	14,070.50
Billy Mayfair	72	71	74	71	288	14,070.50
Brett Ogle	70	75	72	71	288	14,070.50
Steve Gotsche	72	70	74	72	288	14,070.50
Michael Campbell	70	73	73	72	288	14,070.50
Anders Forsbrand	74	71	71	72	288	14,070.50
Sean Murphy	71	75	68	74	288	14,070.50

96th U. S. Open

Contestant	Rounds				Total	Prize
Lucas Parsons	75	71	73	70	289	9,918.20
J.L. Lewis	76	69	73	71	289	9,918.20
Bob Ford	69	77	72	71	289	9,918.20
Scott Simpson	70	71	76	72	289	9,918.20
Wayne Riley	73	69	74	73	289	9,918.20
Steve Elkington	72	70	74	73	289	9,918.20
Tommy Tolles	77	68	71	73	289	9,918.20
Corey Pavin	73	70	72	74	289	9,918.20
Kirk Triplett	70	73	72	74	289	9,918.20
Loren Roberts	72	73	69	75	289	9,918.20
Wayne Westner	72	75	74	69	290	6,619.10
Bob Gilder	73	72	75	70	290	6,619.10
Kenny Perry	73	71	75	71	290	6,619.10
Jeff Sluman	70	74	74	72	290	6,619.10
Joey Gullion	73	72	73	72	290	6,619.10
Hale Irwin	72	71	73	74	290	6,619.10
Alexander Cejka	74	70	72	74	290	6,619.10
Michael Bradley	71	74	71	74	290	6,619.10
Kelly Gibson	71	73	71	75	290	6,619.10
Justin Leonard	71	76	67	76	290	6,619.10
Steve Stricker	74	71	75	71	291	5,825.00
Steve Lowery	73	74	73	71	291	5,825.00
Bill Porter	73	75	72	71	291	5,825.00
William Murchison	76	68	74	73	291	5,825.00
*Randy Leen	77	71	70	73	291	Medal
David Gilford	74	69	74	74	291	5,825.00
Dennis Harrington	75	71	71	74	291	5,825.00
David Duval	75	72	75	70	292	5,645.00
Andrew Morse	76	72	74	70	292	5,645.00
Paul Azinger	69	74	78	71	292	5,645.00
Frank Lickliter	75	71	73	73	292	5,645.00
Masashi Ozaki	69	72	77	74	292	5,645.00
Costantino Rocca	71	74	73	74	292	5,645.00
Wayne Grady	71	75	72	74	292	5,645.00
David Ogrin	72	74	72	74	292	5,645.00
Peter O'Malley	75	73	70	74	292	5,645.00
Curt Byrum	70	76	71	75	292	5,645.00
Jim Gallagher, Jr.	71	72	73	76	292	5,645.00
Bob Tway	72	75	68	77	292	5,645.00
*Trip Kuehne	79	69	73	72	293	
Michael Christie	72	75	72	74	293	5,505.00
Ian Woosnam	72	72	74	75	293	5,505.00
*Tiger Woods	76	69	77	72	294	
John Huston	73	72	76	73	294	5,415.00
Kent Jones	71	74	76	73	294	5,415.00
Skip Kendall	77	71	73	73	294	5,415.00
Scott McCarron	72	72	75	75	294	5,415.00
Tom Kite	76	71	72	75	294	5,415.00
Brad Faxon	70	72	76	76	294	5,415.00
Neal Lancaster	74	67	74	79	294	5,415.00
Craig Parry	70	76	75	74	295	5,305.00
Javier Sanchez	71	76	74	74	295	5,305.00
Jack O'Keefe	72	71	76	76	295	5,305.00
Jay Haas	73	72	74	76	295	5,305.00
Anthony Rodriguez	71	77	76	72	296	5,235.00
Tom Pernice, Jr.	74	72	74	76	296	5,235.00
Phil Mickelson	76	71	73	76	296	5,235.00
Jeff Maggert	75	69	81	72	297	5,165.00
Jim Thorpe	75	71	78	73	297	5,165.00
Blaine McCallister	71	75	76	75	297	5,165.00
Philip Walton	69	73	78	77	297	5,165.00
Omar Uresti	76	72	74	76	298	5,105.00
Olin Browne	73	70	76	79	298	5,105.00
Gary Trivisonno	69	75	78	77	299	5,075.00
Mark Wiebe	74	74	75	77	300	5,055.00
*Steve Scott	71	73	81	76	301	
Rich Yokota	79	67	76	79	301	5,035.00
Mike Burke, Jr.	78	70	77	77	302	5,015.00
Shawn Kelly	73	75	79	82	309	5,000.00

Darrell Kestner	77-72 – 149	Francis Quinn	73-77 – 150	David Toms	76-77 – 153
Scott Dunlap	78-71 – 149	Emlyn Aubrey	78-73 – 151	Mark James	75-79 – 154
Jeffrey Julian	74-75 – 149	Barry Lane	75-76 – 151	Steve Flesch	80-74 – 154
Mike Heinen	73-76 – 149	Philip Blackmar	78-73 – 151	*Reid Edstrom	77-77 – 154
Tim Herron	75-74 – 149	Tom Weiskopf	76-75 – 151	Peter Teravainen	75-79 – 154
Paul Goydos	71-78 – 149	David Edwards	72-79 – 151	Brian Henninger	78-76 – 154
Ted Tryba	74-76 – 150	Fred Funk	74-77 – 151	Greg Lesher	81-73 – 154
Mark Calcavecchia	77-73 – 150	Brandt Jobe	75-76 – 151	Paul Eales	74-81 – 155
*Jay Hobby, Jr.	74-76 – 150	John Flannery	76-75 – 151	Tad Holloway	80-76 – 156
Todd Demsey	77-73 – 150	Steve Jurgensen	74-77 – 151	David Frost	78-78 – 156
Duffy Waldorf	73-77 – 150	Mark McCumber	76-76 – 152	Ronald Ewing	80-76 – 156
Ben Crenshaw	80-70 – 150	Brian Gay	75-77 – 152	Darrett Brinker	78-80 – 158
Kent Wiese	77-73 – 150	Scott Gump	75-77 – 152	Ian Baker-Finch	83-82 – 165
Larry Mize	74-76 – 150	Kevin Sutherland	73-80 – 152	Charles Raulerson	83	WD
Darren Clarke	77-73 – 150	Carl Paulson	78-75 – 153	Bernhard Langer	75	DQ
Ty Armstrong	80-70 – 150	Bryan Hughett	76-77 – 153	Grant Waite		DQ

Professionals not returning 72-hole scores received $1,000 each.

*Denotes amateur.

96th U.S. Open Statistics

Hole	1	2	3	4	5	6	7	8	9	10	11	12	13	14	15	16	17	18	Total
Par	4	5	3	4	4	4	4	4	3	4	4	5	3	4	4	4	3	4	70
Steve Jones																			
Round 1	4	5	3	4	4	4	4	4	[4]	4	[5]	5	[4]	4	4	4	[4]	4	74
Round 2	4	(4)	3	(3)	4	(3)	[5]	4	3	4	4	(4)	[2]	4	4	4	3	4	66
Round 3	4	(4)	(2)	4	4	4	4	4	3	4	4	5	[4]	4	4	4	[4]	(3)	69
Round 4	4	5	3	4	4	4	4	4	(2)	(3)	4	(4)	[4]	4	4	4	[4]	4	69	278
Tom Lehman																			
Round 1	(3)	(4)	[4]	4	[5]	4	4	[5]	3	4	4	(4)	3	4	4	4	3	[5]	71
Round 2	[5]	5	3	4	4	4	4	[5]	3	(3)	4	[6]	3	4	4	4	(2)	[5]	72
Round 3	4	(4)	(2)	[5]	4	(3)	(3)	4	3	4	(3)	5	3	4	4	(3)	3	4	65
Round 4	[5]	(4)	3	4	4	(3)	(3)	4	3	[5]	4	[6]	3	4	4	4	3	[5]	71	279
Davis Love III																			
Round 1	[5]	5	3	4	4	4	4	4	3	4	4	(4)	3	[5]	4	4	3	4	71
Round 2	4	5	3	4	4	4	4	4	3	4	4	5	3	4	4	(3)	3	4	69
Round 3	4	(4)	3	[5]	4	(3)	[5]	[5]	3	4	(3)	5	[4]	(3)	4	4	3	4	70
Round 4	4	(4)	3	[5]	4	4	4	(3)	3	[5]	(3)	(4)	3	4	(3)	4	[4]	[5]	69	279

○ Circled numbers represent birdies, □ squared numbers represent bogeys.

Hole	Yards	Par	Eagles	Birdies	Pars	Bogeys	Higher	Average
1	433	4	0	54	303	145	22	4.263
2	523	5	11	188	274	48	3	4.702
3	194	3	0	66	363	93	2	3.059
4	430	4	0	78	325	112	9	4.099
5	455	4	1	42	305	159	17	4.291
6	356	4	0	104	344	71	5	3.956
7	405	4	0	49	341	118	16	4.196
8	440	4	0	37	333	140	14	4.251
9	220	3	0	36	274	190	24	3.391
OUT	3456	35	12	654	2862	1076	112	36.208
10	450	4	0	38	311	162	13	4.288
11	399	4	0	86	301	126	11	4.118
12	560	5	3	157	314	47	3	4.790
13	170	3	0	54	357	101	12	3.135
14	471	4	0	22	314	160	28	4.370
15	400	4	2	57	334	119	12	4.158
16	403	4	1	61	323	114	25	4.198
17	200	3	0	34	301	169	20	3.337
18	465	4	0	26	239	221	38	4.536
IN	3518	35	6	535	2794	1219	162	36.930
TOTAL	6974	70	18	1189	5656	2295	274	73.138

96th U.S. Open
Past Results

Date	Winner	Score	Runner-Up	Venue
1895	Horace Rawlins	173 - 36 holes	Willie Dunn	Newport GC, Newport, RI
1896	James Foulis	152 - 36 holes	Horace Rawlins	Shinnecock Hills GC, Southampton, NY
1897	Joe Lloyd	162 - 36 holes	Willie Anderson	Chicago GC, Wheaton, IL
1898	Fred Herd	328 - 72 holes	Alex Smith	Myopia Hunt Club, S. Hamilton, MA
1899	Willie Smith	315	George Low / Val Fitzjohn / W.H. Way	Baltimore CC, Baltimore, MD
1900	Harry Vardon	313	J.H. Taylor	Chicago GC, Wheaton, IL
1901	*Willie Anderson (85)	331	Alex Smith (86)	Myopia Hunt Club, S. Hamilton, MA
1902	Laurie Auchterlonie	307	Stewart Gardner	Garden City GC, Garden City, NY
1903	*Willie Anderson (82)	307	David Brown (84)	Baltusrol GC, Springfield, NJ
1904	Willie Anderson	303	Gil Nicholls	Glen View Club, Golf, IL
1905	Willie Anderson	314	Alex Smith	Myopia Hunt Club, S. Hamilton, MA
1906	Alex Smith	295	Willie Smith	Onwentsia Club, Lake Forest, IL
1907	Alex Ross	302	Gil Nicholls	Philadelphia Cricket Club, Chestnut Hill, PA
1908	*Fred McLeod (77)	322	Willie Smith (83)	Myopia Hunt Club, S. Hamilton, MA
1909	George Sargent	290	Tom McNamara	Englewood GC, Englewood, NJ
1910	*Alex Smith (71)	298	John J. McDermott (75) / Macdonald Smith (77)	Philadelphia Cricket Club, Chestnut Hill, PA
1911	*John J. McDermott (80)	307	Michael J. Brady (82) / George O. Simpson (85)	Chicago GC, Wheaton, IL
1912	John J. McDermott	294	Tom McNamara	CC of Buffalo, Buffalo, NY
1913	*Francis Ouimet (72)	304	Harry Vardon (77) / Edward Ray (78)	The Country Club, Brookline, MA
1914	Walter Hagen	290	Charles Evans, Jr.	Midlothian CC, Blue Island, IL
1915	Jerome D. Travers	297	Tom McNamara	Baltusrol GC, Springfield, NJ
1916	Charles Evans, Jr.	286	Jock Hutchinson	Minikahda Club, Minneapolis, MN
1917-18	No Championships Played — World War I			
1919	*Walter Hagen (77)	301	Michael J. Brady (78)	Brae Burn CC, West Newton, MA
1920	Edward Ray	295	Harry Vardon / Jack Burke, Sr. / Leo Diegel / Jock Hutchison	Inverness Club, Toledo, OH
1921	James M. Barnes	289	Walter Hagen / Fred McLeod	Columbia CC, Chevy Chase, MD
1922	Gene Sarazen	288	John L. Black / Robert T. Jones, Jr.	Skokie CC, Glencoe, IL
1923	*Robert T. Jones, Jr. (76)	296	Bobby Cruickshank (78)	Inwood CC, Inwood, NY
1924	Cyril Walker	297	Robert T. Jones, Jr.	Oakland Hills CC, Birmingham, MI
1925	*William MacFarlane (147)	291	Robert T. Jones, Jr. (148)	Worcester CC, Worcester, MA
1926	Robert T. Jones, Jr.	293	Joe Turnesa	Scioto CC, Columbus, OH
1927	*Tommy Armour (76)	301	Harry Cooper (79)	Oakmont CC, Oakmont, PA
1928	*Johnny Farrell (143)	294	Robert T. Jones, Jr. (144)	Olympia Fields CC, Matteson, IL
1929	*Robert T. Jones, Jr. (141)	294	Al Espinosa (164)	Winged Foot GC, Mamaroneck, NY
1930	Robert T. Jones, Jr.	287	Macdonald Smith	Interlachen CC, Hopkins, MN

Past Results

Date	Winner	Score	Runner-Up	Venue
1931	*Billy Burke (149-148)	292	George Von Elm (149-149)	Inverness Club, Toledo, OH
1932	Gene Sarazen	286	Phil Perkins Bobby Cruickshank	Fresh Meadows CC, Flushing, NY
1933	Johnny Goodman	287	Ralph Guldahl	North Shore CC, Glenview, IL
1934	Olin Dutra	293	Gene Sarazen	Merion Cricket Club, Ardmore, PA
1935	Sam Parks, Jr.	299	Jimmy Thomson	Oakmont CC, Oakmont, PA
1936	Tony Manero	282	Harry Cooper	Baltusrol GC, Springfield, NJ
1937	Ralph Guldahl	281	Sam Snead	Oakland Hills CC, Birmingham, MI
1938	Ralph Guldahl	284	Dick Metz	Cherry Hills CC, Englewood, CO
1939	*Byron Nelson (68-70)	284	Craig Wood (68-73) Denny Shute (76)	Philadelphia CC, West Conshohocken, PA
1940	*Lawson Little (70)	287	Gene Sarazen (73)	Canterbury GC, Cleveland, OH
1941	Craig Wood	284	Denny Shute	Colonial Club, Fort Worth, TX
1942-45	No Championships Played — World War II			
1946	*Lloyd Mangrum (72-72)	284	Vic Ghezzi (72-73) Byron Nelson (72-73)	Canterbury GC, Cleveland, OH
1947	*Lew Worsham (69)	282	Sam Snead (70)	St. Louis CC, Clayton, MO
1948	Ben Hogan	276	Jimmy Demaret	Riviera CC, Los Angeles, CA
1949	Cary Middlecoff	286	Sam Snead Clayton Heafner	Medinah CC, Medinah, IL
1950	*Ben Hogan (69)	287	Lloyd Mangrum (73) George Fazio (75)	Merion GC, Ardmore, PA
1951	Ben Hogan	287	Clayton Heafner	Oakland Hills CC, Birmingham, MI
1952	Julius Boros	281	Ed (Porky) Oliver	Northwood CC, Dallas, TX
1953	Ben Hogan	283	Sam Snead	Oakmont CC, Oakmont, PA
1954	Ed Furgol	284	Gene Littler	Baltusrol GC, Springfield, NJ
1955	*Jack Fleck (69)	287	Ben Hogan (72)	The Olympic Club, San Francisco, CA
1956	Cary Middlecoff	281	Ben Hogan Julius Boros	Oak Hill CC, Rochester, NY
1957	*Dick Mayer (72)	282	Cary Middlecoff (79)	Inverness Club, Toledo, OH
1958	Tommy Bolt	283	Gary Player	Southern Hills CC, Tulsa, OK
1959	Billy Casper	282	Bob Rosburg	Winged Foot GC, Mamaroneck, NY
1960	Arnold Palmer	280	Jack Nicklaus	Cherry Hills CC, Englewood, CO
1961	Gene Littler	281	Bob Goalby Doug Sanders	Oakland Hills CC, Birmingham, MI
1962	*Jack Nicklaus (71)	283	Arnold Palmer (74)	Oakmont CC, Oakmont, PA
1963	*Julius Boros (70)	293	Jacky Cupit (73) Arnold Palmer (76)	The Country Club, Brookline, MA
1964	Ken Venturi	278	Tommy Jacobs	Congressional CC, Washington, DC
1965	*Gary Player (71)	282	Kel Nagle (74)	Bellerive CC, St. Louis, MO
1966	*Billy Casper (69)	278	Arnold Palmer (73)	The Olympic Club, San Francisco, CA
1967	Jack Nicklaus	275	Arnold Palmer	Baltusrol GC, Springfield, NJ
1968	Lee Trevino	275	Jack Nicklaus	Oak Hill CC, Rochester, NY
1969	Orville Moody	281	Deane Beman Al Geiberger Bob Rosburg	Champions GC, Houston, TX
1970	Tony Jacklin	281	Dave Hill	Hazeltine National GC, Chaska, MN
1971	*Lee Trevino (68)	280	Jack Nicklaus (71)	Merion GC, Ardmore, PA
1972	Jack Nicklaus	290	Bruce Crampton	Pebble Beach GL, Pebble Beach, CA
1973	Johnny Miller	279	John Schlee	Oakmont CC, Oakmont, PA
1974	Hale Irwin	287	Forrest Fezler	Winged Foot GC, Mamaroneck, NY
1975	*Lou Graham (71)	287	John Mahaffey (73)	Medinah CC, Medinah, IL
1976	Jerry Pate	277	Tom Weiskopf Al Geiberger	Atlanta Athletic Club, Duluth, GA

Date	Winner	Score	Runner-Up	Venue
1977	Hubert Green	278	Lou Graham	Southern Hills CC, Tulsa, OK
1978	Andy North	285	Dave Stockton J.C. Snead	Cherry Hills CC, Englewood, CO
1979	Hale Irwin	284	Gary Player Jerry Pate	Inverness Club, Toledo, OH
1980	Jack Nicklaus	272	Isao Aoki	Baltusrol GC, Springfield, NJ
1981	David Graham	273	George Burns Bill Rogers	Merion GC, Ardmore, PA
1982	Tom Watson	282	Jack Nicklaus	Pebble Beach GL, Pebble Beach, CA
1983	Larry Nelson	280	Tom Watson	Oakmont CC, Oakmont, PA
1984	*Fuzzy Zoeller (67)	276	Greg Norman (75)	Winged Foot GC, Mamaroneck, NY
1985	Andy North	279	Dave Barr Chen Tze Chung Denis Watson	Oakland Hills CC, Birmingham, MI
1986	Raymond Floyd	279	Lanny Wadkins Chip Beck	Shinnecock Hills GC, Southampton, NY
1987	Scott Simpson	277	Tom Watson	The Olympic Club, San Francisco, CA
1988	*Curtis Strange (71)	278	Nick Faldo (75)	The Country Club, Brookline, MA
1989	Curtis Strange	278	Chip Beck Mark McCumber Ian Woosnam	Oak Hill CC, Rochester, NY
1990	*Hale Irwin (74+3)	280	Mike Donald (74+4)	Medinah CC, Medinah, IL
1991	*Payne Stewart (75)	282	Scott Simpson (77)	Hazeltine National GC, Chaska, MN
1992	Tom Kite	285	Jeff Sluman	Pebble Beach GL, Pebble Beach, CA
1993	Lee Janzen	272	Payne Stewart	Baltusrol GC, Springfield, NJ
1994	*Ernie Els (74+4+4)	289	Loren Roberts (74+4+5) Colin Montgomerie (78)	Oakmont CC, Oakmont, PA
1995	Corey Pavin	280	Greg Norman	Shinnecock Hills GC, Southampton, NY
1996	Steve Jones	278	Tom Lehman Davis Love III	Oakland Hills CC, Birmingham, MI

*Winner in playoff; figures in parentheses indicate scores

96th U.S. Open Championship Records

Oldest champion (years/months/days)
   45/0/15 — Hale Irwin (1990)
Youngest champion
   19/10/14 — John J. McDermott (1911)
Most victories
   4 — Willie Anderson (1901, '03, '04, '05)
   4 — Robert T. Jones, Jr. (1923, '26, '29, '30)
   4 — Ben Hogan (1948, '50, '51, '53)
   4 — Jack Nicklaus (1962, '67, '72, '80)
   3 — Hale Irwin (1974, '79, '90)
   2 — by 11 players: Alex Smith (1906, '10), John J. McDermott (1911, '12), Walter Hagen (1914, '19), Gene Sarazen (1922, '32), Ralph Guldahl (1937, '38), Cary Middlecoff (1949, '56), Julius Boros (1952, '63), Billy Casper (1959, '66), Lee Trevino (1968, '71), Andy North (1978, '85), and Curtis Strange (1988, '89).
Consecutive victories
   Willie Anderson (1903, '04, '05)
   John J. McDermott (1911, '12)
   Robert T. Jones, Jr. (1929, '30)
   Ralph Guldahl (1937, '38)
   Ben Hogan (1950, '51)
   Curtis Strange (1988, '89)
Most times runner-up
   4 — Sam Snead
   4 — Robert T. Jones, Jr.
   4 — Arnold Palmer
   4 — Jack Nicklaus
Longest course
   7,195 yards — Medinah CC (No. 3 Course), Medinah, IL (1990)
Shortest course
   Since World War II
   6,528 yards — Merion GC (East Course), Ardmore, PA (1971, '81)
Most often host club of Open
   7 — Baltusrol GC, Springfield, NJ (1903, '15, '36, '54, '67, '80, '93)
   7 — Oakmont (PA) CC (1927, '35, '53, '62, '73, '83, '94)
Largest entry
   6,244 (1992)
Smallest entry
   11 (1895)
Lowest score, 72 holes
   272 — Jack Nicklaus (63-71-70-68), at Baltusrol GC (Lower Course), Springfield, NJ (1980)
   272 — Lee Janzen (67-67-69-69), at Baltusrol GC (Lower Course), Springfield, NJ (1993)
Lowest score, first 54 holes
   203 — George Burns (69-66-68), at Merion GC (East Course), Ardmore, PA (1981)
   203 — Tze-Chung Chen (65-69-69), at Oakland Hills CC (South Course), Birmingham, MI (1985)
   203 — Lee Janzen (67-67-69), at Baltusrol GC (Lower Course), Springfield, NJ (1993)
Lowest score, last 54 holes
   203 — Loren Roberts (69-64-70), at Oakmont CC, Oakmont, PA (1994)
Lowest score, first 36 holes
   134 — Jack Nicklaus (63-71), at Baltusrol GC (Lower Course), Springfield, NJ (1980)
   134 — Chen Tze-Chung (65-69), at Oakland Hills CC (South Course), Birmingham, MI (1985)
   134 — Lee Janzen (67-67), at Baltusrol GC (Lower Course), Springfield, NJ (1993)
Lowest score, last 36 holes
   132 — Larry Nelson (65-67), at Oakmont CC, Oakmont, PA (1983)
Lowest score, 9 holes
   29 — Neal Lancaster (second nine, fourth round) at Shinnecock Hills GC, Southampton, NY (1995)
   29 — Neal Lancaster (second nine, second round) at Oakland Hills CC, Birmingham, MI (1996)
Lowest score, 18 holes
   63 — Johnny Miller, fourth round at Oakmont CC, Oakmont, PA (1973)
   63 — Jack Nicklaus, first round at Baltusrol GC (Lower Course), Springfield, NJ (1980)
   63 — Tom Weiskopf, first round at Baltusrol GC (Lower Course), Springfield, NJ (1980)
Largest winning margin
   11 — Willie Smith (315), at Baltimore (MD) CC (Roland Park Course) (1899)
Highest winning score
   Since World War II
   293 — Julius Boros, at The Country Club, Brookline, MA (1963) (won in playoff)
Best start by champion
   63 — Jack Nicklaus, at Baltusrol GC (Lower Course), Springfield, NJ (1980)
Best finish by champion
   63 — Johnny Miller, at Oakmont (PA) CC (1973)
Worst start by champion
   Since World War II
   76 — Ben Hogan, at Oakland Hills CC (South Course), Birmingham, MI (1951)
   76 — Jack Fleck, at The Olympic Club (Lake Course), San Francisco, CA (1955)
Worst finish by champion
   Since World War II
   75 — Cary Middlecoff, at Medinah CC (No. 3 Course), Medinah, IL (1949)
   75 — Hale Irwin, at Inverness Club, Toledo, OH (1979)

Lowest score to lead field, 18 holes
    63 — Jack Nicklaus and Tom Weiskopf, at Baltusrol GC (Lower Course), Springfield, NJ (1980)

Lowest score to lead field, 36 holes
    134 — Jack Nicklaus (63-71), at Baltusrol GC (Lower Course), Springfield, NJ (1980)
    134 — Chen Tze-Chung (65-69), at Oakland Hills CC (South Course), Birmingham, MI (1985)
    134 — Lee Janzen (67-67), at Baltusrol GC (Lower Course), Springfield, NJ (1993)

Lowest score to lead field, 54 holes
    203 — George Burns (69-66-68), at Merion GC (East Course), Ardmore, PA (1981)
    203 — Chen Tze-Chung (65-69-69), at Oakland Hills CC (South Course), Birmingham, MI (1985)
    203 — Lee Janzen (67-67-69), at Baltusrol GC (Lower Course), Springfield, NJ (1993)

Highest score to lead field, 18 holes
    Since World War II
    71 — Sam Snead, at Oakland Hills CC (South Course), Birmingham, MI (1951)
    71 — Tommy Bolt, Julius Boros, and Dick Metz, at Southern Hills CC, Tulsa, OK (1958)
    71 — Tony Jacklin, at Hazeltine National GC, Chaska, MN (1970)
    71 — Orville Moody, Jack Nicklaus, Chi Chi Rodriguez, Mason Rudolph, Tom Shaw, and Kermit Zarley, at Pebble Beach (CA) Golf Links (1972)

Highest score to lead field, 36 holes
    Since World War II
    144 — Bobby Locke (73-71), at Oakland Hills CC (South Course), Birmingham, MI (1951)
    144 — Tommy Bolt (67-77) and E. Harvie Ward (74-70), at The Olympic Club (Lake Course), San Francisco, CA (1955)
    144 — Homero Blancas (74-70), Bruce Crampton (74-70), Jack Nicklaus (71-73), Cesar Seduno (72-72), Lanny Wadkins (76-68) and Kermit Zarley (71-73), at Pebble Beach (CA) Golf Links (1972)

Highest score to lead field, 54 holes
    Since World War II
    218 — Bobby Locke (73-71-74), at Oakland Hills CC (South Course), Birmingham, MI (1951)
    218 — Jacky Cupit (70-72-76), at The Country Club, Brookline, MA (1963)

Highest 36-hole cut
    155 — at The Olympic Club (Lakeside Course), San Francisco, CA (1955)

Most players to tie for lead, 18 holes
    7 — at Pebble Beach (CA) Golf Links (1972); at Southern Hills CC, Tulsa, OK (1977); and at Shinnecock Hills GC, Southampton, NY (1896)

Most players to tie for lead, 36 holes
    6 — at Pebble Beach (CA) Golf Links (1972)

Most players to tie for lead, 54 holes
    4 — at Oakmont (PA) CC (1973)

Most sub-par rounds, championship
    124 — at Medinah CC (No. 3 Course), Medinah, IL (1990)

Most sub-par 72-hole totals, championship
    28 — at Medinah CC (No. 3 Course), Medinah, IL (1990)

Most sub-par scores, first round
    39 — at Medinah CC (No. 3 Course), Medinah, IL (1990)

Most sub-par scores, second round
    47 — at Medinah CC (No. 3 Course), Medinah, IL (1990)

Most sub-par scores, third round
    24 — at Medinah CC (No. 3 Course), Medinah, IL (1990)

Most sub-par scores, fourth round
    18 — at Baltusrol GC (Lower Course), Springfield, NJ (1993)

Most sub-par rounds by one player in one championship
    4 — Billy Casper, at The Olympic Club (Lakeside Course), San Francisco, CA (1966)
    4 — Lee Trevino, at Oak Hill CC (East Course), Rochester, NY (1968)
    4 — Tony Jacklin, at Hazeltine National GC, Chaska, MN (1970)
    4 — Lee Janzen, at Baltusrol GC (Lower Course), Springfield, NJ (1993)

Highest score, one hole
    19 — Ray Ainsley, at the 16th (par 4) at Cherry Hills CC, Englewood, CO (1938)

Most consecutive birdies
    6 — George Burns (holes 2–7), at Pebble Beach (CA) Golf Links (1972) and Andy Dillard (holes 1–6), at Pebble Beach (CA) Golf Links (1992)

Most consecutive 3s
    7 — Hubert Green (holes 10–16), at Southern Hills Country Club, Tulsa, OK (1977)
    7 — Peter Jacobsen (holes 1–7), at The Country Club, Brookline, MA (1988)

Most consecutive Opens
    40 — Jack Nicklaus (1957-96)

Most Opens completed 72 holes
    33 — Jack Nicklaus

Most consecutive Opens completed 72 holes
    22 — Walter Hagen (1913-36; no Championships 1917-18)
    22 — Gene Sarazen (1920-41)
    22 — Gary Player (1958-79)

96th U.S. Open Championship
Oakland Hills Country Club
June 13-16, 1996